Outrageous!

Outrageous!

Unforgettable Service . . .
Guilt-Free Selling

T. Scott Gross

AMACOM
American Management Association

New York • Atlanta • Boston • Chicago • Kansas City • San Francisco • Washington, D.C.
Brussels • Mexico City • Tokyo • Toronto

This publication is designed to provide accurate and authoritative information in regard to the subject matter covered. It is sold with the understanding that the publisher is not engaged in rendering legal, accounting, or other professional service. If legal advice or other expert assistance is required, the services of a competent professional person should be sought.

Library of Congress Cataloging-in-Publication Data

Gross, T. Scott.
    Outrageous! : unforgettable service—guilt-free selling / T. Scott
Gross.
        p.   cm.
    Includes index.
    ISBN 0-8144-7986-3
    1. Selling.   2. Customer services.   I. Title.
HF5438.25.G758   1998
658.8'12—DC21   98–5611
                                                                    CIP

Printing number

10   9   8   7

*This book and everything I do is dedicated
to the one I love . . . Melanie.
(But you can call her Buns!)*

CONTENTS

FOREWORD

Don't buy this book unless you want to change the way you think about doing business. Maybe you shouldn't even buy this book unless you are willing to rethink the way you think, the way you relate to your family, even who you are. Positively Outrageous Service isn't so much an idea as it is a way of life.

Business, that is, work, is supposed to be fun. If that doesn't sit well with you, better spend your bucks on more appropriate reading, perhaps something on Trends in Service in the Twenty-first Century . . . (yawn).

POS is fun. And when you are doing it right, work is supposed to be fun. Work should fill you with joy and make you feel good.

What if Shirley MacLaine is wrong and you really do only go around once? Wouldn't you like to get it right this time?

Outrageous!

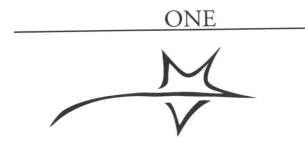

ONE

GUILT-FREE SELLING

"As long as employees
see selling as a thinly veiled
opportunity to bend a customer over
the cash register so that he can be frisked,
the really good folks will continue to avoid
selling like the plague."

Employees don't sell. They hate the idea. They don't know how. Who could blame them? The boss blames the employee. The employee thinks the boss is a con artist. The employee is right.

Selling doesn't come in a can. Great selling is a by-product of great service.

Selling, like all work, is supposed to be joyful. That's not to say that everything should be a party; only that if you wake in the morning and hate the thought of going to work, you're not doing it right.

The same is true for being sold. If a customer leaves feeling "sold" rather than "served," someone goofed in a major way.

We put the little Mooney smoothly down on the runway at Dallas Love Field and taxied to the ramp at AMR Combs. Five, not one, two, three, or four, but five ramp folks came out to park our plane. The one woman among them guided our plane to its spot with arm motions that looked borrowed from the Cowboy cheerleaders. I wanted to yell, "Give me an S, give me a C . . ." and spell out my name in recognition of a picture-perfect arrival.

"What's the occasion?"

"It's summer. We're not busy and thought you would enjoy a real reception!"

We did.

Now fuel for the little Mooney runs about $2.40 a gallon and we needed nearly sixty to top the tanks. Go ahead, do the math. Pretty expensive fill-up, wouldn't you say? But the price was totally lost in the fun of the moment.

"How long are you going to be with us?"

"Just long enough to buy a couch."

"You'll never get a couch in that Mooney! Do you need transportation?"

"Yes, please. It should only take an hour." I was hoping to get the crew car but those are often reserved for the crews of the big jets, the ones that order fuel by the pound, not Mooney drivers who fill their sports planes by the gallon and take up valuable ramp space.

"Well, take the crew car."

We borrowed the crew car and headed to The Arrangement, a favorite Dallas stop.

Elizabeth is anything but a salesperson. Yes, she probably gets paid on commission and, yes, in a furniture store there are plenty of opportunities to sell. But we've never felt "sold" by Elizabeth.

When we first called to inquire about a desk that was featured in a *Texas Monthly* ad, Elizabeth didn't ask what was our budget or otherwise attempt to qualify us. Instead she set about qualifying the desk! She wanted to make certain that our new room would be the correct size for the furniture.

"Fax me a diagram of your new office space and I'll have a suggestion or two ready when you come in."

POS Point: Remember to qualify the product as well as the customer!

Wow! That's nice. We thought we might buy a desk. Elizabeth totally changed the relationship. She was interested in fixing up our office. The desk had become incidental to the process!

A couple of weeks later when we visited the store for the first time, Elizabeth pulled our file and offered a couple of suggestions for arranging the room. Imagine that! Elizabeth had no guarantee that we would actually show up, yet she had gone to the trouble to prepare a floor plan. Pretty neat, huh?

Now here's the selling-service part. Both layouts included furnishings beyond the desk that we were interested in seeing. But the intention clearly was not to sell more "stuff." It was to show us how to put together a complete office that would serve us well. No pressure to buy more; only a suggestion about how we might use the space.

So we bought the desk, a chair, and a lamp or two. And there was the bookcase and, oh, yes! I should probably mention the entertainment center. We bought more furniture in an hour than we had purchased in our twenty-one years of marriage. But we bought the furniture—Elizabeth didn't sell it. We *bought* a complete home office. We weren't *sold* anything.

And that's why we were on our way back to The Arrangement to be their first customers on that hot summer day.

We bought the couch right away.

We had seen the couch in the store's flyer that had tickled our mailbox and fancy a few days earlier. We decided to add an occasional chair. That's what they call them, occasional chairs. Frankly, at those prices, that occasional chair had better be a full-time chair! We added a table, actually three, to complete the set. Then Elizabeth mentioned, suggested, said, "Do you know what would really make this? A woven rug. I've got one on sale that might look perfect. Would you like to see it?"

POS Point: Selling complete solutions yields bigger sales and happier customers.

Well, looking never hurts and darned if it didn't look really good. Elizabeth discovered that it was the least expensive of the three that she had brought for us to try against the couch.

But we bought it; Elizabeth didn't sell it. Elizabeth *presented* us with a look, a completed room setting, a feeling. We could see ourselves cuddling on that big overstuffed couch, watching football in the fall or curled in its corners reading late into the night. Elizabeth didn't sell us anything.

Great selling . . . isn't. Great selling is great service.

When we returned home, there were two sketches on our fax machine. Elizabeth had taken the dimensions of our room and laid out the furniture to make certain that it would fit. In fact, she sent two entirely different floor plans and suggested that we hand our favorite to the delivery crew when the furniture arrives.

That's service. Even though we had just spent another small pile of dollars, we left feeling served rather than sold.

~∽∾∽~

The trick is to translate that sales approach to your business. It's not difficult, and it will take a little practice; but, more important, it may force you to take a new look at the process of selling.

There are psychological instruments that predict whether or not an applicant has that killer instinct, that mental toughness and hunger that we mistakenly think is at the heart of a great salesperson. I think that kind of thinking is what Zig Ziglar would call stinkin' thinkin'. Maybe it worked in the old days, but no longer.

POS Point: Don't pitch . . . present. Showmanship is an art form of selling.

We have one speaker's bureau that works with us occasionally that I know would be more successful if they weren't quite so hungry. The bureaus that have the highest closing ratio when selling us and Positively Outrageous Service seem to be those who put the consumer first and make it their first priority to find the perfect speaker for the audience instead of selling any speaker the meeting planner will buy.

In sales, hunger doesn't get you sales. In sales, hunger keeps you hungry because it keeps you from putting the customer first. When the customer is more important than the sale, magic happens. I don't remember who said it, but it is better to make a customer than a sale because customers come back again. Happy customers become your marketing program. Wounded customers become mere price shoppers, spoiling the market for all of us.

How do you turn selling into service? Follow these three important steps:

1. Reward high-pressure service instead of high-pressure selling.
2. Teach guilt-free selling.
3. Be an example of servant leadership and guilt-free selling.

Here is the context that separates high-pressure selling from guilt-free selling. The high-pressure salesperson looks at a customer and says, "This guy has another dollar. I wonder what I could do to get it?" The guilt-free seller looks at the same customer and thinks, "This guy still has a problem or two that needs solving. I wonder what I could do to be the one who can solve it?"

In the end the results are the same. You get the customer's last dollar.

The difference? One went for the dollar, the other went for the customer. It isn't really a matter of content, only context. My guess is that customers can sense that subtle distinction.

POS Point: Sell a customer, get paid. Serve a customer, get paid again and again!

My son Rodney is perhaps the world's greatest practitioner of servant selling.

He once came to the house excited over landing a job with one of San Antonio's pre-eminent auto dealerships. Rodney was all of eighteen and really turned on by the job offer. He had been buying and selling cars since he was fifteen. Cars were his life and he was good, really good. He intuitively knew every sales technique in the book, and he had the tenacity of a Doberman when it came to negotiating a purchase.

Rodney raided his savings to buy a complete new wardrobe. He was bound and determined to look and sell like the very best. Now here was a kid that an employer would die for.

The excitement was quickly extinguished.

After the first day on the job, my kiddo came dragging into the house. "Dad, you won't believe how they treat people over there. They'll cut your throat for a dollar. They fight over who's up. And when it's a young couple who just want a car to get them to work, they sell them a car and a payment that they know they won't be able to keep. They talk bad about customers and each other in the worst possible way. They're slimy and I don't like being around them.

"I can't sell someone a car that I know is wrong for them or that I know they can't afford. To these guys it's just another sale, a commission hit in their wallet."

Two days later Rodney returned the new clothes. A few years later he opened his own retail store, and now he can outbuy and outsell the sleazeball salespeople he left behind.

One day a woman walked into the newly opened Rod's Stereo Sounds, my kiddo's business in Kerrville, Texas. (I'm a pretty proud dad over the fact that he never took a penny of Mom and Dad's money to open his business. Pretty cool in these days of "let Daddy pick up the tab.")

The woman had $3,500 cash in an envelope and a list of stereo equipment that could outfit a theater. "Can you get me everything on this list for $3,500?" she asked my son.

Rodney looked at the list, did a quick mental calculation, and said, "I think so. This is pretty sophisticated equipment. You must be a serious music lover."

"Actually," said the lady, "this is a list of stereo equipment that my ex-husband left to me. It was damaged by lightning, and this is the insurance money they gave me to replace it."

Rod asked if, like her ex-husband, she was an audiophile. No, she just listened to the radio and an occasional CD. She was worried about fitting everything into her new, but small, apartment.

"I can sell you a terrific system for less than half of what you have in that envelope. You don't need all that equipment for your apartment. You can use the rest of the money for something that's more important to you."

What would the average salesperson have done? He probably would have sold her the entire list and surprise! The total would have been within pennies of $3,500.

"I can't believe you're doing this," said the woman.

"That's because you don't understand how my business works. You see, I give you great equipment at good prices, follow up with a little service, and you tell everybody in town!"

"There's a book out called *Positively Outrageous Service*. My new boss gave it to me to read before starting to work.

And I think what you are giving me is what they call POS. I'll bet you've even read the book. The author lives here in the Hill Country. Do you know him?"

(I'll bet you know the next line in this story!)

The first week or so Rodney was in business, a local businessman stopped by the store.

"I think my stereo is shot, but since I probably won't keep this car long, I'd like to stay under $500 or $600."

Rodney suggested that the stereo might be fine. It could be the speakers that were the problem. He offered to put in a pair of speakers that he had on sale for $129, saying that if that wasn't the solution, he would remove them at no charge.

The speakers turned out to be the problem, and the customer left ecstatic about having spent far less than the $600 that many salespeople would have found reason to charge.

What makes this story better is that not all that many folks in town are aware that Rodney is my son. Who told me this great servant-selling story? It wasn't Rodney—it was someone who had heard the story from someone who had heard the story.

GIVE ME THE FAX!

Joanne Schlosser, president of Dynamic Presentations, wrote in amazement over the service she received from a telemarketer soliciting her long-distance telephone business. (Oh, no! Not another one!) Actually, this one used a little POS to his advantage.

Writes Joanne, "instead of the usual blather, this guy actually asked me some questions about my business. When he learned that Dynamic Presentations provides training in customer service, he asked if I had seen a recent article on the subject in a national magazine. When I said I hadn't, he offered to fax it to me. Was that empowerment? I was blown away that a young telemarketer would do that.

"It was an awesome article, and I switched carriers as a result!"

And that is the true value of making a customer instead of booking another sale—people talk. And the talk is positive talk that spreads like wildfire when folks hear about an honest salesperson who knows that the key to sales lies in the willingness to serve.

One hallmark of big business is the tendency to put a sales pitch in a can. It makes sense as long as you don't look too closely.

We look at the sales process and realize that adding a slice of cheese, selling a shoe tree with each pair of shoes, or adding the famous dealer prep charges can, over the course of a year, make a substantial difference to the bottom line. That's the first-blush view. Look closer and the picture changes.

Add enough pressure to the process, make the customer feel like a number, embarrass your team by making them use goofy sales ploys and what do you really accomplish? Read on and find out.

After the movie *Jurassic Park* hit the theaters, a supervisor of a national chain of home furnishing stores actually required employees to answer the phone saying, "Thank you for calling (I'll leave the name out to protect the totally silly). Welcome to our Jurassic sale! Have we got a dino of a deal for you!"

Any idea why employees aren't just thrilled out of their gourds to sell?

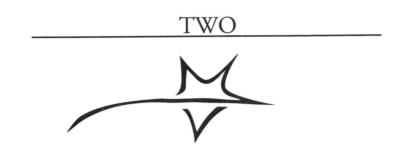

TWO

POSITIVELY OUTRAGEOUS SERVICE!

If you haven't figured out this POS stuff by now, it is not coming. If you have, you know that POS is about loving your customers unconditionally, and you have to be prepared for customers, guests, patients, clients, or whatever, to be pretty darned unlovable.

I admit to taking the easy way out.

I'm telling a Southwest Airlines story.

THE CHRISTMAS MAN

First the scene. Christmas Eve at a busy SWA gate. The gate agent is suffering from a cold; she is away from her family for the holiday season and feeling as miserable as the weather.

This is a story about angels. Two of them. One is an "angel unaware" named Rachel. The other is named McDonald.

Now, in the words of Angel Rachel:

> I looked up and saw the sweetest-looking old man standing with a cane. He walked very slowly

over to the counter and in the faintest voice told me that he had to go to New Orleans. I tried to explain to him that there were no more flights that night and that he would have to go in the morning. He looked so confused and very worried.

I asked if he had a reservation or if he remembered when he was supposed to travel, but he seemed to get more confused with each question. He just kept saying, "She said I have to go to New Orleans."

It took a while but finally I was able to discover that this old man had been dropped off at the curb by his sister-in-law on Christmas Eve and told to go to New Orleans where he had family. She had given him some cash and told him to "just go inside and buy a ticket." When I asked if he could come back tomorrow, he said that she was gone and that he had no place to stay. He then said bravely that he would "wait right here until tomorrow."

Naturally, I felt a little ashamed. Here I was feeling sorry for myself about being alone for Christmas, when this angel named Mr. McDonald was sent to me as a reminder of what being alone really meant. It broke my heart to see him standing there.

I told him not to worry, that we would get everything straightened out. Cynthia, another agent on duty, helped book him a seat on the earliest flight the next morning. We gave him a senior citizen's fare, which left him a little extra money for traveling. About this time, he started looking very tired and I stepped around the counter to ask quietly if he was all right. That's when I noticed that his leg was wrapped in a bandage. He had been standing on it the whole time, holding a plastic bag full of clothes.

I called for a wheelchair. When the wheelchair came, we both stepped around to help him in, and noticed a small amount of blood on his bandage. I asked how he had hurt his leg and he explained that he had just had bypass surgery and that an artery had been taken from his leg. Can you imagine. This man had heart surgery, and shortly afterward had been dropped off at the curb to buy a ticket with no reservation to fly to New Orleans alone?

I had never really had a situation like this, and I wasn't sure what I could do. I went back to ask my supervisors, Kathy and Mercedes. When they had heard the whole story, I asked if we could find a place for him to stay. They both said absolutely.

We gave Mr. McDonald a hotel room for the night and a meal ticket for dinner and breakfast. When I came back out, we got his plastic bag of clothes and cane together and gave the nice World Services' employee a tip to take him downstairs to wait for the shuttle. I bent down to explain the hotel, food, and itinerary again while I patted him on the arm. I promised him that everything would be just fine.

As he was about to be wheeled away, he said, "Thank you," bent his head, and started to cry.

I cried, too.

When I went back to thank Kathy, she just smiled and said, "I love stories like that. He is your Christmas man."

THE REAL POSITIVELY OUTRAGEOUS SERVICE

Positively Outrageous Service is a story. It is about the top line and the bottom line. It is the story of how great servers love their customers unconditionally and put big money on the bottom line. But they profit in other ways, too. When an organization adopts Positively Outrageous Service heart, line, and sinker, there are other changes that are often difficult to describe but impossible to miss.

Positively Outrageous Service is as much about who you are as it is about what you do.

The nice thing is that when you change what you do, it changes who you are.

Random and unexpected. Out of proportion to the circumstance. Invites the customer to play or otherwise become highly involved. Creates compelling, positive word-of-mouth. It is the service story that you can't wait to tell.

We discovered Positively Outrageous Service when we attempted to run a franchise fried chicken joint in a small town in Texas. I had been the national director of training and knew that I knew more than anyone on the planet about running one of those small, efficient money machines. I had a wealth of hands-on operations to ensure the deal. Opening our store was a hands-down, sure-fire, no-miss, winner of a deal. Well, wrong-o! We had the best location in town. Plenty of pre-opening publicity. A town that had been asking for years for the company to open an outlet so they wouldn't have to wait for infrequent trips to San Antonio for their fix of this delicious product.

We opened with a bang. Make that a double bang. It took so long to count the money I almost didn't have time to order product.

Every week the numbers got smaller and smaller as the novelty of a new store in a small town began to wear off. In a matter of two months, there was plenty of time to count the money, just not much that needed counting.

We had the best product, packaging, price, and place. What we didn't have were customers. There were days when we ate more fried chicken than our customers did. The only good thing about that was we never had to ask the question, "What's for dinner?" We knew what would be for dinner. Chicken. Fried. Swell!

And while what was for dinner wasn't much of an issue, we occasionally wondered how old it was. We ate lots of chicken.

One holiday season while we were still trying to figure out how to get out of this mess, we got the bright idea to give away chicken. Why not? We certainly weren't selling it!

Actually, it happened one afternoon as my wife and I were driving home. I said, "We sure are lucky," as I held her hand across the console of the Jeep.

It took her a moment to catch the drift of the conversation. When you are buried in debt and smelling like shortening, good luck is usually not your top-of-mind position. She caught on, "We are?"

"Sure! We've got a great son and each other. We have our health and our tomorrow. There are a lot of people who are far less fortunate."

Melanie got the hang of it, and we started listing our blessings. The list turned out to be pretty long, especially when you realize that we didn't have to take up space by mentioning that albatross of a business that owned us.

"Why don't we share some of our good luck this Christmas? We could give away five hundred chicken dinners on Christmas Day to those who are truly hungry!"

"But we can't pay for the chicken that we're selling!"

"See? Perfect! It will be just like we've been doing all along only a whole lot more fun!"

For whatever dumbheaded reason, we decided to go for it. To make a long story short, it turned around our business because it turned around our way of thinking.

It wasn't price, product, packaging, or place that caused people to eat at our place. It was, we later discovered, the promise that if they'd choose to do business with us, they would feel good. Positively Outrageous Service is all about making people feel good that they decided to do business with you.

We discovered that customers don't want to be surprised

when it comes to the product or service they are seeking. They want, and need, to be able to depend on getting what they want, how they want it, at the price they expect to pay, day in and day out. No surprises.

But customers do like surprises of the pleasant variety, and therein lies the secret of Positively Outrageous Service. You do not deliver POS every time for every customer. Once in a while, every now and then, you surprise them, pleasantly.

The theory behind POS has a name, something to the effect of random reinforcement for consistent behavior. You'll remember this from Psych 101.

You have a few more stories to read before you really begin to catch on. At first you will be certain that POS comes in only one of two categories: Either you are crying or giving stuff away. Keep reading and you will discover that there is much more to POS than crying or giving stuff away.

You do have to give something away, but not stuff, not money. To practice POS, you have to give away creativity, fun, compassion, and, once in a while, a little "stuff." For POS, you give away the moment and throw away the rules.

Here's one of those "give-away-stuff" stories that will make your boss cringe, but it's a great story. So read on!

CHAIN SAW

Jim Weber, owner of the Coast to Coast store in Clark, South Dakota, has an understanding of customer service that goes beyond the initials POS. When he discovered that he did not carry a critical part needed for one of his customers to complete a plumbing project, Jim headed out the door and straight to a nearby True Value store. You know what he did. He brought back the part and confirmed a customer for life!

At the Coast to Coast store in Ridgecrest, California, Duane Wildes had just taken over as store manager when a customer came in asking about a chain saw part that was supposed to be on order. Duane told the customer that he would check on it and have an answer the next day. Upon checking, he was unable to determine what had happened to the order. When the customer returned the next day, he became understandably upset upon hearing the news.

Determined to satisfy the customer, Duane did the unthinkable. He went to the shelf, picked a new 14-inch Homelite saw, and gave it to the customer. He told the customer that he didn't want to lose his business and that the saw was on the house!

Later that same day, the customer returned and purchased $1,200 in merchandise. In the year following, the customer spent $4,000!

POS? Yes! Good business? Definitely!

> *Random and unexpected. Out of proportion to the circumstance. The customer is invited to play or is otherwise highly involved. It creates compelling, positive word-of-mouth. POS is the service story that you can't wait to tell.*

Reread the stories above and see if they meet the definition. They do!

If POS had to be defined in fewer words, we would have to use "WOW" and "random." The idea is to do something so grand, so big and unexpected, that when you hear the story, you've just gotta say "WOW!"

The other half of the definition involves the idea of randomness. Randomness gives us the element of surprise. If the customer is expecting it, you may have good, even great service. Unless there is a sense of surprise, it isn't Positively Outrageous Service.

We've debated the issue of whether or not it's a good idea to tell people that you practice POS. On one hand you run the risk of removing the surprise. But remember, as long as POS is delivered on a random basis, the surprise is still there. Still, be cautioned that posting a sign or wearing a pin that boasts that you practice POS will indeed raise expectations and should be done only if you can actually deliver on a promise as positive as POS.

What should a customer expect of someone or an organization that professes to practice Positively Outrageous Service? They should expect that the staff is empowered to have fun, be creative, show compassion, and, in general, put the customer first. They should expect to be served by a staff, which is in turn served by management, in a Positively Outrageous fashion.

Above all, when you promise POS, you are implying that you have taken great care to hire people who are willing and able to love their customers unconditionally.

> *Random and unexpected, out of proportion to the circumstance, POS invites the customer to play and creates compelling, positive word-of-mouth.*

I caught a wonderful photo on the front page of our local newspaper taken by photo pro Ken Schmidt. The photo is of a local high school football team (Tivy High School). Not your average action shot that features one fat kid clobbering another. Nope, this one shows the entire team walking along the sideline, shaking hands with the fans and thanking them for attending the game and showing their support!

When was the last time you saw a megabuck pro team do this? Never? Well, imagine that!

I'd call this surprising display of sportsmanship and hospitality a pretty fine example of POS! Random and unexpected. Out of proportion to the circumstance. Invites the customer to play or be otherwise highly involved and definitely creates compelling, positive word-of-mouth!

AADVANTAGE!

My friends at Southwest Airlines hate it when I admit to occasional lapses of loyalty and fly with the other guys—but only where SWA doesn't go!

One of the best examples of POS came courtesy of the computer system that keeps American Airlines flying. We had been in Dallas speaking when an ice storm of major proportion hit the city. There had to be nearly an inch of ice on everything. Now, ice and airplanes aren't a favorite combination. As you might imagine, DFW turned into ZOO. Very little was either coming or going. Every half hour or so they would manage to squeeze off a flight going to one of the few places in the region that was not ice-covered. In fact, while paying my dues in traveler's hell, I heard this interesting announcement:

"If you are in the gate area and have a ticket to Baton Rouge or somewhere else that you are not going to today, we invite you to board at this time."

We accepted the delay like good sports, called the folks in Mt. Pleasant, Texas, where I was scheduled to speak that evening, and weighed the odds of making it by car. We bet on the airline and made it. Not by a lot, but we made it!

Several days later, I received a letter from Michael Gunn, vice president of marketing for American:

> Last Saturday's storms in the Dallas/Fort Worth area brought hail that damaged several of our American Airlines and American Eagle aircraft at DFW. Unfortunately, as a result, many of our flights were delayed or canceled. This situation affected many passengers who, like you, traveled through or from DFW late Saturday or Sunday.
>
> While we can't control the weather, we would like to apologize for any inconvenience this situation may have caused you. And, because we appreciate your patience, we have credited your AAdvantage account with 500 bonus miles as a token of our appreciation.
>
> At American, we want to make sure that every

flight you take with us is a pleasant experience. We regret that the weather doesn't always cooperate.

Brilliant! POS!

At the Drury Inn in St. Louis, a couple who had just checked in received a message that their first grandchild was on the way in Lexington, Kentucky. The staff arranged a "watch party" with other guests joining in the wait. "This helped make the event even more exciting," wrote the new grandparents. "The next day we received a beautiful congratulations card and candy from the manager!"

If that isn't POS, what is?

When I first wrote about POS, I discovered that a friend of a friend had a friend of a friend who might know someone at Southwest Airlines. And maybe, just maybe, they could get someone there to write an endorsement for the jacket. Naturally, this first-time author was thrilled at the prospect.

We bundled up the manuscript and sent it to the friend of a friend, as close to the SWA target as possible, who in turn passed our bundle along until it finally, amazingly made it to the top. If you are thinking it went to Herb Kelleher, think again. I said that my package made it to the top. Herb is just another pretty SWA face. The real power is in the unlikely presence of Colleen Barrett, "Goddess of All Things SWA." (I may be off slightly on the title, but I'm at least close!)

The days turned into weeks and no word from SWA. Go figure. They probably get a jillion such requests every week from real authors. Why would they pay any attention to me?

When the phone rang, Mom picked it up and said, "T. Scott Gross and Company, this is Betty!" She listened for a moment, then covered the phone as if the Pope was calling and whispered loudly, "Quick! It's someone from Southwest Airlines!"

"This is Sherry Phelps," came the abbreviated introduction from somewhere in Dallas. "Are you the guy who wrote *Positively Outrageous Service?*"

"Yes, ma'am." I swallowed hard.

"We have to get one thing straight before this conversation goes one word further."

Oh, geez. Not only do they not like the book, they've found something bad and I'm going to get sued!

"Have you been up here studying our company?"

I was sooooo relieved! Of course I had studied their company! Not by sneaking around their corporate digs, but from the back of the plane on a million flights to everywhere! I told her and waited a long, long millisecond.

"Good!" The voice was instantly cheerful. "How do I get ten thousand copies?"

AHHHHHHHHHHHHHHH!!!!!

So I'll tell another story that just happens to mention Southwest Airlines. Hey! It's not my fault they practice POS.

Jill M. wrote to share this one:

> I was at the Sacramento Host Hotel last week delivering a training program, trying without much luck to get a document printed from a computer disk and faxed to the East Coast. The catering manager of the hotel overheard me relate my frustration to a colleague. He took it upon himself to escort me to the hotel offices where we tried in vain to convert my document on the hotel computer. Not giving up, he called every airline buddy he had over at the terminal until he found one that could help.
>
> Of course, it was good old Southwest Airlines willing to help me out! The operations supervisor at Southwest met us in the terminal, took us to his office, and set me up with a computer that had compatible software. Once printed, he offered to fax my document, but the employee from Host insisted that he would do the faxing. Now we were getting positively, positively outrageous!
>
> When I asked if they had ever heard of your

book, the Southwest employee said, "Sure, we read that book in our training programs." That did not surprise me, knowing all the great things you've said about Southwest. I've sent the Host employee a copy of your book so he can recognize his already outrageous behavior.

SURPRISE!

POS is not rocket science. It only requires a willingness to serve and an inspiration to go one step further than expected.

C. Johnson of Shakopee, Minnesota (would I make up a place named Shakopee?), was surprised when she stopped at her local Amoco station and was "thrilled" when the attendant on the full-service island offered her and her daughter a free beverage. What was the cost to the station? And what was it worth in terms of positive, compelling word-of-mouth? Mrs. Johnson sent me a wonderful handwritten letter. Imagine how many people she told!

"You had better believe that the next time I needed gas, I went to the same station," she said, claiming that now she is "hooked" on Positively Outrageous Service.

Getting hooked is the whole idea. You never know when POS will strike, so you have to keep coming back again and again.

The principle is simple—surprise them once in a while and they'll never know exactly when it will happen again. So, the only way to get a little POS is to come in a lot.

HALO!

My spelling checker picked up halo as hello. Good point. Once a customer has received Positively Outrageous Service, you get the benefit of the halo effect. When the customer deals with you the next time, even if you only manage to deliver your usual consistently wonderful service, the glow of the previous POS experience will surround the moment. One shot of Positively Outrageous Service colors subsequent visits. It's the gift that keeps on giving!

POS WORKS!

A few years ago we brought POS to Blair Hotels in Cody, Wyoming. That same year they reported an amazing increase in revenues (which they kindly attributed to POS).

But what about the tough times? Well, last year, due to an epidemic of road construction, the town fathers reported an 8 to 15 percent drop in sales, but not at Blair Hotels! Their positive service attitude held up both spirits and sales and allowed Blair Hotels to finish the season ahead of the previous great year.

If you are ever in Cody (and you should go), stop at a Blair Hotel for a great night's sleep and a healthy dose of POS!

LITTLE TOUCHES

The Ritz Carlton in Hawaii so delighted one of our readers that he suspected that their landscape figured prominently in their service strategy. Now, it's pretty tough to surprise a customer with shrubbery but . . .

The first thing I noticed was the valet parking. At the valet station stood three very athletic-looking attendants. I watched as a customer approached the captain. He immediately handed the keys to one of the attendants who took off like a rocket to get the car. There were several obstacles, in particular a row of hedges and a flower bed.

Instead of going around the hedges and following the sidewalk, he left the sidewalk, leaped the hedges, and ran through the flower bed being careful not to step on any of the flowers.

Then it happened again with a different attendant. As I watched, it became apparent that hedge-leaping was standard operating procedure.

On the surface, this was just great customer service. After I thought about it, I realized that it was brilliant customer service, even Positively Outrageous Service. Running around the building, jumping hedges, tripping through the flower bed was probably not even the quickest way to retrieve cars. But when these guys ran, the customers watched. And they said, "WOW!"

I wonder if the hedges were intentionally planted to be leapt. About that, I would not be surprised!

And then there is the server in Baton Rouge who takes her camera to work on busy days to take pictures of her customers and their families. She requests a business card and in a few days, and at her own expense, mails them both the print and the negative.

Would that get you to say WOW? Where would you want to sit when you returned to dine?

BREAK!

Jim and Maggie Hayes were here for a visit so we flew the little Mooney to San Angelo for lunch. (Jim and Maggie are working with us on a project to create a training program for the general aviation industry, and we needed to do a little research.)

At lunch, Jim ordered a Dr. Pepper.

"Sorry! No Dr. Pepper! I'll bring you a Pibb. That's a genetic clone of the good doctor. Order the spicy chicken and you'll never know the difference."

Jim ordered the spicy chicken. As the waitress left the table, she verified our orders, "You get the pig dish with the fattening rice. You're undecided, you ordered both sweet and sour. Yours is the one with all the veggies and you (she looked at Jim), you, honey, are the spicy one!"

That's playful. That's the kind of service that comes naturally to some, but most can be taught. We'll learn how to play with the customer in a later chapter. Now, back to the studio!

WHEN LIFE GIVES YOU LEMONS

A day or so after the Toro Company was added to our spring speaking schedule, our media director plopped a book onto my desk and said, "You'd better read this. It looks like your client is an author."

Making the Grass Greener on Your Side is the product of Toro CEO, Ken Melrose. I read the book and it's a good one. Of two-hundred-plus pages, there was one story on a single page that told me more about Toro and its leader than all the other pages combined. There, on page 81, I learned the real secret behind the phenomenal success of Toro.

In the summer of 1987, the headquarters building had been damaged by local flooding, not really what you would call major, but certainly a real inconvenience with carpet pulled up and offices in disarray.

Mel Foss was a senior buyer at the time and was meeting with the president and vice president of one of the company's major suppliers. Mel tried to keep the discussion on focus, a task that was made more difficult by the sticky floors and general mayhem of an office trying to pull itself together. To add to the distraction, there was a ruckus outside the office door.

Mel started to get up to handle the distraction when the door to his office opened and in walked an executive-type man who cheerfully greeted the group and began serving fresh lemonade and cookies.

When the man left the office, the visiting president asked, "Who was that guy and does he do this kind of thing often?"

The visitor was CEO Ken Melrose, who had returned

early from a national show to show his support of the home office crew.

Mel reports that the conversation immediately turned away from the inconvenience of the flooding to the importance of leadership. Says Mel, "We all took something away from that momentary encounter."

And so can we. Positively Outrageous Service only happens for customers when the folks on the inside are served with a healthy dose of POS from time to time.

RELAX!

Sandra Green wrote from the Residence Inn in Torrance, California, to tell about a little POS delivered in person by her general manager, David Zimmerman.

When asked how he was enjoying his stay, a long-term guest reported that the Residence Inn was just like home except that he really missed his favorite recliner. In a casual conversation, Sandra mentioned the comment to Zimmerman who, "didn't waste time but went right out and found a good deal on a recliner. He put the chair in the guest's room. When Mr. Guest walked into his room that evening, he couldn't believe his eyes!"

"In all his years of traveling," said the guest, "no one had ever responded to a simple comment quite like that!"

> *Random and unexpected, out of proportion to the circumstance, invites the customer to play or become otherwise highly involved and creates compelling, positive word-of-mouth. And, we might add, creates an incredible sense of loyalty.*

Surely, for the price of a recliner, David Zimmerman had purchased a customer for life, and not just for the Residence Inn in Torrance, but for a Residence Inn anywhere this guest might travel.

Okay. One quickie from that same Residence Inn.

This particular inn had a very extended-stay guest—four years! They must be doing something right!

At Christmastime, while the guest was away at work, the staff installed a fully decorated Christmas tree, complete with a case of the guest's favorite beer. By the way the beer was replenished every six weeks by a Santa working on special assignment!

WRAP

Positively Outrageous Service is all about wrapping an experience around the service transaction. As you read on, you'll bump into lots of ideas; some you can use whole, but most will need a little adapting. As you read these examples of service excellence, avoid discounting them just because they may not come from your industry. In fact, pay extra attention to ideas that may never have been tried in your business. These are the ideas most likely to surprise. After all, humor is nothing more than the unlikely juxtaposition of two or more incongruent ideas.

In plain English, people laugh or smile when you make them look at their world in a way they did not expect.

So, put on those rose-colored glasses and learn to look at service as an opportunity to make someone smile. If you are a bottom-line type, wrapping an experience around a service transaction builds sales. If you are a top-line type, wrapping an experience around a service transaction makes the day go fast. Either way, you can't lose when you deliver a healthy dose of Positively Outrageous Service!

Just like in the "Naked City," in every audience, there are a million stories. Here is one:

Liz R. couldn't wait to share her story of Positively Outrageous Service. Liz was living in Boston in 1974 when there was a fire in her apartment. Nearly everything she owned was destroyed by the blaze, including her new Hitachi TV. The fire completely melted the cabinet of the set but, much to everyone's surprise, when she turned it on, it worked!

Liz was so surprised that she wrote the company to say thank you for a great product.

From her letter, the folks at Hitachi tracked Liz to her workplace. When a surprised Liz answered their call, they invited her to bring the burned set to a local department store where they had arranged for her to exchange it for a brand new set!

Would you call that Positively Outrageous Service? I would. But I would also call it heads-up marketing. Think about it. For the manufacturer's cost of a television set, Hitachi got a wonderful marketing tool (the burned but working set) plus incredible word-of-mouth advertising from a very satisfied customer.

In fact, look at the last few stories and what do you see?

You could see several nice people who spotted an opportunity to serve and acted. You could also see several smart marketers who saw an opportunity to get incredible, positive word-of-mouth.

The odd thing about Positively Outrageous Service is that no matter what the motive the result is the same—happy customers who tell others.

If you are naturally nice, you are probably already doing something that is close to Positively Outrageous Service. Well, keep being nice. Your good works will come back to you.

On the other hand, if you are the scum of the universe, do what I am teaching you. Good works come back to whomever sent them out. Whether you are selfish or selfless, Positively Outrageous Service is for you!

I HAVE A PROBLEM WITH CANADIANS!

In today's mail I found these interesting stories, proving that you never know whom you might reach and verifying a startling truth about Canadians: They think service in their country is awful and they are wrong!

Marilyn, project coordinator of the Victoria, British Columbia Hospitality Award, sent the following wonderful examples of Positively Outrageous Service. If you haven't been to Victoria, B.C., you are missing one of the most beautiful places and some of the nicest people on the planet!

Joanne, concierge at the Ocean Pointe Resort, received a special City of Victoria medallion for her Positively Outrageous Service when a guest who had reservations at the resort was unable to get from the airport due to a shortage of rental cars.

Joanne sprang into action and located an available car from a local Toyota dealership. She then rousted her husband and sent him to pick up the guest. Her husband then quickly took the guest to the dealership, so the guest could still make his "tee time!" See? Not one friendly Canadian, but two!

When a couple from the United States visited Victoria, they decided to round out their trip by experiencing a neighborhood pub. They called the Monkey Tree Pub and were greeted by Dana who immediately picked up their accent, recognizing that they were from "down sooth."

A true ambassador, Dana waited at the pub, even though her shift had ended, to make sure that the couple were "properly welcomed" and introduced to local Victorians.

That's POS with a Canadian accent!

Here's a sweet one.

Norm Ingalls, owner of Maple Leaf Gifts in Victoria, received the Victoria Hospitality Award when two visiting seniors stopped in his store. Norm recognized the women as being British and engaged them in conversation of days gone by. Seventy-two-year-old Joyce reminisced about her friendship with George, an American gunner flying for the RAF in World War II. She had traveled across Canada thinking about how interesting it would be if she were to run into her old friend.

In a matter of minutes, a resourceful Norm Ingalls had George on the line and Joyce was connected with a beau she hadn't seen in over fifty years!

CHAMPAGNE?

Tony Colao is a bit of a romantic. Anyone with his passion for music just has to be. Tony is a graduate of a small upstate New York college where he met and then married his college sweetheart. Marrying shortly after graduation, it was no coincidence that their twenty-fifth reunion and twenty-fifth wedding anniversary fell within a few days of each other last summer.

Tony decided to "put on the dog" and arranged for a special surprise at a hotel on Mirror Lake (near Lake Placid). Tony booked the second-best room they had. (Tony may be a romantic, but he's not extravagant!) Still, this second-best room weighed in at $290 per night. Tony plunked down a night's deposit and promised to settle at checkout.

Included in the package was a bottle of champagne and flowers, perfect for a twenty-fifth wedding anniversary.

It was no surprise the two-level suite overlooking the lake was truly awesome. And, again, no surprise, champagne and flowers awaited. Actually, it was champagne and a plant, which was more than Tony had bargained for. He read the ho-hum note that was attached. It read, "Enjoy your champagne and flowers."

The happy campers hung out the "Do Not Disturb" sign and enjoyed a quiet weekend.

So far there wasn't much to be said about the service. Tony and his sweetie never bothered the hotel with requests, electing to enjoy the local restaurants rather than test room service or the hotel dining room.

Now the surprise.

When they visited the front desk to check out, a drole clerk said that the bill had already been paid.

Now there's a surprise! On the way home, Tony decided that it had to have been his family who had sleuthed out his hideaway and arranged the treat. He called his sister to ask exactly who had paid and how they knew his plans. During the conversation she asked, "How did you like the champagne and plant?"

Get it? Someone at the hotel decided that since there was already champagne and flowers in the room, there was no need to supply any more. Just attach the hotel note to the goodies already available and the job is done!

I could tell you how the story ends but just for grins, you make the call. How would you handle the situation? The hotel is nearly 400 miles from Tony's house. Got any ideas?

For now, think about this: What are you doing to make your customers laugh, smile, or shed a tear of joy?

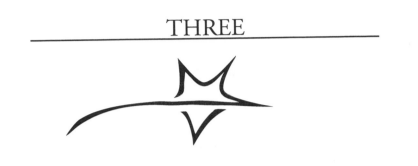

THREE

FOUR STEPS: HARD SERVE, SOFT SELL

O kay, it's no-brainer time! What are the steps to service in any organization?

STEP ONE: ESTABLISH RAPPORT

We often use the term "greet the customer." What we are really doing is establishing rapport, which has a deeper meaning than simply saying "Hello." Establishing rapport requires that you do something to encourage the customer to trust you. You can establish rapport by offering a small token of hospitality such as a place to sit, a cool drink on a hot day, or a friendly greeting when things are busy. Building rapport is more than a matter of trust; it is a matter of letting the customer know that he or she has your attention and respect.

To get off on the right foot with a customer, you must demonstrate up front that you respect them as a human being. "May I help you?" may be an accepted way to initiate a transaction but it falls miles short of establishing rapport.

How do servers everywhere tell customers to go straight to hell? They ignore them. When you treat someone as if their time has little value, you are essentially saying that they have little value. Waste *my* time and all the slick promotions in the world aren't going to get you my business.

Martha Vang of Sante Fe, New Mexico, told us an interesting and all-too-typical story. Melanie and I were flying into Sante Fe to collaborate with Martha's best friend and husband, Fred. Martha is probably the world's most gracious hostess, and her home is a living work of art. When Martha invited us to dinner, we knew we were in for a treat.

Treating us like honored customers (See? The word really does substitute nicely), Martha began the meal by carefully selecting the ingredients. The entrée was going to be roast pork and Martha set out to find the best roast in all of Sante Fe. She stopped at a butcher shop known to carry the freshest meat and poultry. When Martha entered the store, she was surprised to discover that it was apparently deserted. Stepping further toward the counter, she spotted the lone butcher on duty talking on the phone.

She waited five minutes and then pecked gently on the glass of the butcher case. The butcher looked up, noticed that he had a customer, and signaled to let her know that he saw her.

Five, ten, then fifteen minutes more, a total of twenty long minutes passed, about fifteen of which Martha would not have invested were we not coming to dinner. Finally the butcher emerged, apologizing as he walked behind the meat case.

"Sorry, I was on the phone with the owner. We're having a little problem with profits."

Duh!

To establish rapport, you must have a plan to approach the customer. If you have to run, then run. Whatever you do, signal right up front that the customer is important by respecting his or her time.

Last week I stopped to purchase a mirror for our remodeled bathroom. No big deal. I had called in the measurements, promised what time I would arrive to pick it up, and as promised, appeared right on schedule. That was my part of the bargain.

When I walked in and identified myself, the gentleman behind the counter said, "Sorry, we've been busy and haven't had time to cut your mirror."

Think for a moment. What had to have happened was that other business had been put ahead of mine. They knew when I called in the order what time it needed to be ready. They knew then how much business was ahead of me, so obviously, they took other work ahead of mine. Okay, I can handle that.

Twenty minutes later the mirror was ready. Just as they were about to present my bill, the phone rang. And the clock continued to tick away my afternoon. Ten minutes later the counterman returned with the bill saying, "Sorry. That guy calls here all the time. He never seems to know what he wants."

What happened here? Simple. Other customers were allowed to jump in ahead of me.

Always take customers in the exact order that they (or their work) arrive. If the telephone rings, answer it, of course, but let the caller know if there are other customers ahead of him. The same is true in reverse. If a customer walks in and you have a customer on hold, explain the serving order. Nice people don't mind waiting their turn, and no one likes being, as the kids say, "dissed," by your allowing other customers, or work, to jump in ahead of them.

~⌒∾⌒~

I was crunched for time and arrived at the airport not a minute too soon. A client had arranged for me to pick up my tickets at the counter.

Shifting impatiently from one foot to the other, I waited with the other refugees, watching the clock tick ever closer to boarding time as the line inched slowly forward.

From the side of the counter, a huffing, puffing skycap wheeled a baggage-laden cart to the counter. He had a huge, red-faced man in tow. The skycap explained that "Red" had to catch the 1:45 flight and needed to be checked in quickly.

Well, la-de-dah! 1:45? The same flight that I—and half the line—was waiting on!

When it was my turn, I gently pointed out that, from my vantage point, it had appeared that the best way to get preferential service is to tip the skycap a couple of bucks, sort of a "go-to-the-head-of-the-class" card.

I also pointed out that this is just plain wrong.

(It's also a stupid way to lose a customer.)

POS Point: Show respect for your customer by respecting customer time.

There is another unexpected opportunity to establish rapport, and that is those instances when it is clear from the beginning that you are not going to make a sale.

I was waiting in my son's store to take him to lunch when an older gentleman came in, cellular phone part in hand.

"I have been to two other stores looking for this part. The last store sent me here." He looked at his shoes while handing over the part to one of the young men behind the counter.

"Sorry, sir. This is a Mitsubishi part. We can't even order parts for this particular phone. The nearest authorized dealer is in San Antonio," smiled the young man from behind the counter.

Haven't you been in a similar situation? You left on what you thought would be a simple mission to find a seemingly innocuous part and wound up stopping at half the stores on the planet? What started as a quick trip to the store became an odyssey of Homeric proportions.

I knew that, for this gentleman, he was living one of those stories. Something simple had turned into a project.

At lunch I mentioned this missed opportunity to my kiddo, the world's most customer-focused sales guy. He nearly levitated out of his seat, instantly jumping up to try to recapture the moment, simultaneously realizing that the moment had passed.

"Ohhh, noooo!"

It wasn't a huge goof. Pretty normal for most businesses, just not Rod's place.

You make the call. How should the customer have been handled?

Answer: The customer should have been told that even though they do not carry parts for that phone, if he wouldn't mind waiting, they would be happy to call and try to locate the part for him so that he would be sure to win on the next stop.

They could have gone even further, all the way to Positively Outrageous Service, and volunteered to have their courier pick up the part on the next run from San Antonio, which would save the customer a 120-mile round trip. This would have given the customer another opportunity to stop in the store and would have been a definite WOW! If you got this kind of extra-mile service on a product that you didn't buy at this store, imagine how confident you would feel about making future purchases here.

Of course, while they were on the phone tracking the part, they may have discovered that the customer was about to renew the contract for service. They may have been able to make a sale right on the spot.

Another rapport builder is to get out from behind the counter! Think about how awkward you feel at the doctor's office when you are forced to deal with someone seated behind a 4-foot counter. Makes you feel really separated, doesn't it? It's even worse when they show further contempt by forcing you to talk through a 4-inch hole cut in a glass divider. It's pretty impersonal, isn't it?

Smart operators get out from behind the counter and

shake hands with the customer. If the customer is carrying packages, take them. Greet and meet right at the door. Heck, meet 'em in the parking lot if you have the time! Your hospitality won't be misinterpreted if you remember to treat the customer like a guest.

STEP TWO: DISCOVER THE PROBLEM

All business is about problem solving. My house needs to be painted. My coat needs to be cleaned. My family is hungry. My dog should be fixed.

The second step is often boiled down to a single, "May I help you?", or as we say in Texas, "May ah hep ya?" The true service professional goes much deeper. Here we introduce the concept of the whole project. You can't offer a complete solution until you have discovered the problem—all of it. (Some folks may be more comfortable stating Step Two as "Discover How You Can Help.")

Customers often ask for one thing when they need another. Worse, they often ask for a partial solution because they are unaware of what it will take to completely and satisfactorily solve the problem.

For example, a man asks a lumber dealer for a two-by-four. You could sell him the board and he would leave perfectly satisfied, although not loyal. Or you could ask what kind of project he is working on. If he tells you he's building a deck, you have an opportunity to mention that perhaps he would rather have treated lumber and maybe a can of sealer. He may need decking screws or a blade for the saw. This guy might even appreciate the name of a good carpenter!

The same could be true at a restaurant. Let's say that a customer orders a dry bagel and a cup of coffee. You could deliver the goods, and the customer would be perfectly satisfied. But what if you said, "Sounds like you're watching your weight." And the guest replied, "Yeah, and I hate eating such a boring breakfast, but that's the way a diet goes."

What if you offered jelly for the bagel (since there is no fat in jelly) and perhaps skim milk to make the coffee more pleasant? Now you've demonstrated that you have the customer's best interest in mind. Now you are moving the customer toward loyalty.

Each customer sell-serve situation should come equipped with a semiscripted list of qualifying questions that help you qualify the product or service, not the customer. The customer qualifies for at least some level of service simply by honoring you by walking through your door.

Qualifying questions can be as simple as, "Hi! What kind of project are you working on today?" Your list of qualifiers may need to be more involved if you are offering a complicated or highly customized product. When you must ask extensive or personal qualifying questions, ask first for permission.

"I want to make sure that I can help you with just the right solution. May I ask you a few questions to be sure we're on the right track?"

Even when selling larger ticket items of the "cold-call" variety, it is still important to request and receive customer permission before probing for details. Ask for permission to ask and stand by to be amazed at how cooperative customers can be!

When you are asking questions with the intent of setting an appointment, avoid those goofy hard-sell either/or questions designed to force the customer to choose. Customers are smart enough to see a contrived question coming from a mile away. Never ask, "Would eight o'clock on Tuesday be okay, or would you rather see me at ten on Friday?" What two-year-old doesn't recognize that for what it really is?

Instead ask, "When would you like to meet?" and be professional enough to handle an answer like, "I'm really not interested in meeting any time soon."

At the top of your list of questions, ask what general benefits the customer expects. This may seem obvious, but the answers will frequently be surprising.

We talk to many clients about presenting at their conferences and seminars. One of the questions we ask is, "What do you expect to be the result of our presentation?" Sometimes they say they want the group to go home with a list of concrete ideas for implementing Positively Outrageous Service and Guilt-Free Selling. Other times they are looking for humor and not a lot more.

"Give them something to think about, but keep it light. You're speaking after dinner, and you follow a magician." Sheesh!

Ask the customer something on the order of "What do you want this product to do for you?" If you are selling hardware and they are looking at a faucet set, easy installation may be high on their list and not on your list at all. The only way to find out how to satisfy the customer is to ask!

Later, you'll learn that products and services that are limited in some way automatically assume a higher value in the eyes of the customer. (All value lies in the eyes of the customer!) Exclusive products are often so attractive that customers buy simply because they are afraid of missing out.

One of the best ways to get a customer's attention is to say up front that you may not be able to help them. Customers are used to salespeople trying to make a sale at all costs, even if it means trying to fit a size 10 foot into a size 8 shoe.

They are blown away when you say, "If you don't mind, let me ask you a few questions to see if we will be able to help you."

I can't tell you how many custom video production projects I've landed by telling the customer up front that, "We have a great track record for producing training programs that work. I'm not certain that we would feel comfortable producing the program that you have outlined in the request for proposal. We wouldn't want to be associated with a production that looked pretty but failed to do any real training. Let's look a little closer and we'll make a suggestion for a product that will do what you want it to do. Or we can recommend a production house that might be better suited for the job."

If you really are the expert, don't be afraid to say "no" to the customer when saying "no" is to their benefit. Not only is this the right thing to do, but by saying "no" you only add to your exclusivity. Unlike all the other companies that will do anything just to make the sale, you are doing the right thing to make a customer!

STEP THREE: OFFER A COMPLETE SOLUTION

We've sort of been talking about this, but now, let's look just a bit deeper. Sometimes offering a complete solution requires a little digging or perhaps a bit of anticipating guests' needs. For example, let's say you have a guest check into a hotel and it's very late. A sharp desk clerk might ask if he wants a late checkout or a wake-up call. If possible, the clerk would put the guest in a room away from morning traffic.

Or what about a young couple, the wife obviously pregnant, looking at a two-seat sports car. Does this make sense?

Offering a complete solution is an expression of the ultimate in customer service. It also happens to be a very good way to sell more. The size of the transaction is often not so much a measure of your ability to sell as it is a measure of your willingness to serve!

When you are offering a complete solution, one that serves the customer as well as sells the product, you and the customers are partners, not adversaries. When you have offered the perfect solution and the customer has been educated well enough to recognize that fact, there is absolutely no need to close the sale. When the perfect solution is at hand, the sale is a foregone conclusion. At this point, closing the sale is nothing more than taking the order.

If you have to "close" the sale, you have not served the

customer. With a well-served customer, closing the sale is nothing more than the next step in solving the problem.

STEP FOUR: CEMENT THE RELATIONSHIP

Most organizations are satisfied if they can get employees to simply thank the customer, and in many cases, that's all there is time to do. What we are really after is not a simple, mumbled "Thank you." No, what we want to happen is for customers to recognize, to mentally take notice, that they have just received superior service and that there is a solid reason to return.

"Y'all come back now, ya heah?" might do the trick. But, probably not.

Something has to happen that tells the customer that the act of walking out the door does not terminate the relationship. Something has to happen that assures the customer that the server's parting words will not be, "Next!"

"Mrs. Ramirez, I hope you enjoy that new computer. If you have any trouble at all, call this special number and ask for me. I'll be happy to talk you right through it."

"Mr. Gross, we changed the oil, replaced an exhaust bracket that was under warranty, and checked the seal on the left wing tank. But if you wouldn't mind, after you have a few hours on the engine, taxi over anytime so we can make a quick check that everything is in order."

"We appreciate your business. If you get home and that pizza isn't every bit as good as I described it, call and we'll deliver your usual order, no charge."

Now tell me that there isn't anything you can say to your customers that would cement the relationship.

One Step Into the Cement

Have you ever given in to the temptation to write your initials in wet cement? When the boys poured Mom's driveway, there was quite a bit of posturing over who would get to sign the job. There was even some discussion as to whether or not it might be fun to sit in the wet stuff. (Common sense and modesty prevented the sitting but not the signing.)

Customers are a bit like wet cement. Because we don't often see them every day, we are only as good as their last experience. We were talking yesterday about the food at a restaurant in San Antonio and realized much to our surprise that it had been over ten years since we had eaten there. Think about it. Our impressions of that restaurant are a decade old, and yet today they continue to shape our decision to eat there—or not.

The question is simple. Do we sign our names with pride as we send our customers out the door, or do we squat on the experience, risking that they won't come back for a decade, maybe forever?

As we say in the speaking business, "You are only as good as your last speech."

What are you doing to ensure that every customer leaves with a lasting impression to bring them in again when they next think of you?

Remember Me?

If there is a single way to cement a relationship with a customer, it must surely be the promise that they will be remembered. There is nothing—not quality, not price, not convenience—that will draw a customer like the promise of being remembered.

I like to eat at the Cowboy Steakhouse in Kerrville, Texas. It's my favorite place on the planet. Is the food good? Of course! And the service is always first-rate. Is it the best restaurant anywhere, even the best in Kerrville? Who knows! All I can tell you is that I like it. And if you show up, knock on my door, and want to take me to dinner, you can bet I'll ask for the Cowboy Steakhouse.

Why? Probably for the silliest of reasons—they remember me. I may not be famous in your town (heck, I'm not famous in my own). But I am famous at the Cowboy Steakhouse (everybody is!), and that's where I like to eat. I can count on a hug from Lorrie, and I know that Nancy will remember that I want the chicken, I don't want foil on the baker, and that a gallon of water will just get me started.

We flew into Cincinnati to visit my grandmother and called the folks at Thrifty for a car. We hadn't planned on stopping, but we were ahead of schedule and flying east of our intended route to avoid bad weather. So we had no reservations. No problem. The folks at Thrifty came through. What made the transaction special was Cathy. Several years ago I spoke to the Thrifty annual convention, and they bought a bunch of the original *Positively Outrageous Service* books. I signed the books, had a great time speaking to the crowd, and, like too many engagements, went about my merry way.

Cathy was walking by the counter just as the customer service representative asked my name.

"Scott Gross," I replied.

Cathy stopped, smiled, and said, "Would that be T. Scott Gross?"

"Yes, ma'am, although the T is silent," I grinned at the thought that someone would remember me from four years earlier.

"I loved your book!"

"Thanks! That always makes me feel special. Being remembered is the best compliment of all."

When we said our good-byes and stepped out to find the economy car that we had rented, there waited a jazzy, berry-colored convertible, no extra charge.

I don't expect special treatment. In fact, it's a little embarrassing to be given red-carpet treatment for what seems to be no reason at all. Hey, I was paid to speak to Thrifty. I already got mine and here they were treating me like visiting royalty.

I've washed more cars than I've rented! But the real treat was not in the jazzy car, it was in being remembered.

If you want to make customers feel special, remember them.

People like to do business with people who remember them and attempt to respect their special needs and tastes. If remembering is the best thing you can do, forgetting must be the worst.

I was speaking in Tennessee some years ago. It was one of those two-day deals for a client who had little or no budget. They were doing everything possible to be absolutely certain that I earned my then meager fee. The meeting planner asked me if I would be willing to emcee their awards banquet.

"Sure! It will give me something to do. My pleasure," I replied.

Later that afternoon, as I passed one of the association members in the hall, he said, "I hear you're doing a comedy routine tonight!"

"I am?"

Well, I raced to find the meeting planner. I was blown away when I saw a copy of the agenda, which announced that I would be doing a comedy routine at the awards banquet.

When I mentioned that she had only asked me to emcee, she rather sheepishly replied, "Sorry. Guess I forgot."

So much for remembering. I nearly ran to my room to create my comedy routine, all the while wondering what else she may have forgotten to tell me.

That night I was introduced by one of the board members, who was so fascinated with the idea of a comedy routine that he felt compelled to tell a few "jokes" during my introduction. He had found a joke book, not a very good one, and seemed determined to read stale jokes until he landed a big one, which as it turned out, never happened.

Finally, with the audience nearly comatose, I was introduced and started my routine. The audience had almost rejoined the living when I came to the end of my torture and started to introduce the evening's entertainment.

I was then passed a handwritten note stating that the entertainer was still putting on her costume and that I should "stretch." Stretch? I was relieved to have made it as far as I did and now I had to "stretch?" Give me a break!

I stretched. The audience was getting restless.

Finally, the door opened and in rushed a middle-age woman carrying a boom box the size of a house. She handed me an introduction to read.

It seems that I was introducing Miss Tennessee Nineteen Eighty-Something. I read and introduced simultaneously, Miss Tennessee (surprise), who was about to entertain us with a tap and baton routine. (Be still my heart. And I thought I had the tough duty!)

I stumbled through the intro just in time to hand the mike to the woman with the boom box. She placed the mike in front of the tape player and cranked the volume into overdrive. And as the music screeched and blared, the door flew open to reveal Miss Tennessee decked out in a red-and-white sequined majorette outfit complete with white boots and tassels. She was greeted by thunderous silence.

Just as I had decided that things couldn't get any worse, the meeting planner's genetic predisposition for forgetting details reared its ugly head again.

Tap dance . . . carpet.

Tap dance . . . carpet.

Notice anything unusual?

Our meeting planner had neglected to order the dance floor and now Miss Tennessee Nineteen Eight-Something was about to commit suicide on carpet.

Remembering the details is one of the best ways to cement a relationship. Forgetting the details can quickly destroy any sales-service relationship. It's your choice!

You don't have to remember their name. Remember anything and you'll thrill the average customer. Remember their car, their hat, their accent, or their order and you've done all that is necessary to cement the relationship.

TRY IT!

Let's take a look at how a complete service routine might unfold, using a situation that is typical to the ones we are most likely to see on any day, anywhere.

Rapport: "Hi! Looks like you've got a plumbing project!"

"Yeah, the old tub is about to give up the ghost."

Discover: "So are you going for a short-term fix or a long-term solution?"

"I thought I would slap in a new faucet and maybe look at resurfacing the bottom."

Solve: "As long as you're going that far, for not much more you could install a new, modern tub. I could show you a couple that are really simple to install. Plus, we have a clinic coming up in a couple of days if you think you'll need a pointer or two."

(Customer decided on a new tub.)

"Okay, we've got the tub, faucet set, drain hardware—that should just about do it. Do you have caulk and what about the wall around the tub? Is it plastic or tile?"

"Plastic."

"Then it shouldn't be any problem. This new tub has an extra high splash guard so it should fit right over your current wall cover for a nice smooth fit."

Cement: "If you have any problems, just give me a call and I'll help you any way I can. Thanks for coming in. I'll look for you when you decide to tackle the rest of the bathroom!"

Let's try another one—same principles, different situation.

     Rapport: "Hi! I'm Fred and I'll be your server tonight! And you must be . . . ? Wait! Don't tell me! I'll guess. Charles and Diana?"

"How did you know!? Must have been the crown!"

"Exactly! And I'm the Queen Mother!"

     Discover: "Well, okay, your Royal Highness. Is this a special occasion or are you just sneaking out of the palace for a quiet evening?"

"Actually, we have a big presentation tomorrow and we thought this might be a good place to work out our plan."

     Solve: "Then what you need is peace and quiet. I'll be back in a flash to get your order, and you can count on me to handle refills and details without another word. How's that?"

"That sounds wonderful!"

"When you give me your order, be sure to include a dessert choice. That way you won't hear another word from me."

     Cement: (After dinner) "Good luck on that presentation! I'll expect a full report when you visit us again. And if you did good, I may find something special in the dessert department as a reward!"

Okay, we'll admit it. That may have been a little corny. On the other hand, wouldn't you like to be on the receiving end of that kind of service?

Any transaction, any one at all, can be successfully completed by following the four steps: rapport, discover, solve, and cement.

For more T. Scott Gross . . . www.tscottgross.com

FOUR

THAT'S WHY THERE'S HELL!

There are three things you don't know about handling complaints.

1. Customers usually want less than you think.
2. Customers who have never had a problem are not as loyal as customers who have had a problem that was successfully resolved.
3. Customers who take the time to complain want to make things better.

Look closely at these three points. If you have a policy to do whatever it takes to make things right when things go wrong, simply asking the customer what it is that would make things right yields surprising results. They ask for less than you would have settled for after a negotiation.

Customers who have never had a problem are not as loyal as customers who have had a problem that was successfully resolved. Did you get that? Read it again to be sure! This is so powerful that it's almost worth screwing things up just so you can fix them!

Think about it. If you always deliver on your service promise, how will the customer know that you are not just *consistent*? How would the customer discover that you are *insistent* that the customer's needs be fully and fairly met? You have to have a screwup so you can fix it, demonstrating your sincerity about delivering a quality product and service.

The tough question is, "If this is so obvious, why are so many customer complaints so poorly handled?"

The answer is fear. Fear that the customer is trying to rip you off. Fear that someone will have to take the blame and that that someone might be you.

Employees often think that their job is to protect the company from the customer. Plus, they often believe that complaints are a sign of failure rather than an opportunity to grow. And none of this will change unless it is both communicated and demonstrated by top management. Who would risk stepping out of the box to resolve a customer complaint if they thought that doing so would get them zapped?

> **POS Point: The least expensive way to resolve a complaint is to apologize and ask the customer what would make things right.**

FOUR STEPS TO SERVICE RECOVERY

Surprise! If serving the customer is nothing more than solving a problem, it stands to reason that handling a complaint involves the same basic steps of sales and service. Complaint resolution is a matter of the following:

> **Establish rapport:** Let the customer know up front that you are on their side. This is more than an apology, but that's a start.
>
> **Discover the problem:** Ask the customer to describe the problem exactly—just listen.
>
> **Offer a complete solution:** Ask the customer what they

think is the right solution. Agree, and then up the ante to prove that you are serious.

Cement the relationship: Apologize again, and tell the customer what will be done to prevent a reoccurrence.

If you need a simpler rule for complaints, let it be this: Do whatever it takes to make things right when things go wrong—no matter what.

A customer with a complaint is asking you to help them remain a customer. Complainers are your most loyal customers. They want to continue to do business with you. If they didn't, they would walk across the street and be done with you. Customers who complain are giving you a chance to set things right. Don't blow it.

Complaints are opportunities that you probably haven't seen. If you saw them and failed to act, you don't deserve to have customers who are nice enough to volunteer their help. Hey! It's a pain in the yaha to go to the manager and register a complaint.

What if the manager treats you rudely? What if the manager's idea of fixing a complaint is climbing someone's clock? What if you complain and from then on the staff treats you like dirt? Nope, the easiest way out is out. Just leave. Don't rock the boat, and be sure to tell everyone you know about how badly you were treated.

No, complainers are friends. Just try to keep your list of this kind of friend as short as possible.

Establish Rapport

Right up front say that you are sorry. You don't have to have details. If the customer is upset, you're upset. Period. Let the customer know right up front that you are on their side. Let them know that this is not an adversarial situation. Tell them that you want to hear all the details, and then, this is important, get angry *with* them—not at them!

It is very difficult to pick a fight with someone who is angry about the same thing as you. When the customer says, "I'm really mad about this. You guys did me wrong!", you reply, "I hate it when people treat me poorly. Let's get this straightened out right this minute!"

I've tried this on customers, getting so seemingly angry that they've attempted to calm me down, telling me that it isn't that big of a deal!

Discover the Problem

Now is the time to listen, really listen. Take notes. Ask for more details. Make it absolutely clear that the customer has your undivided attention. By the way, if the complaint involves an employee, ask that employee to take a break or leave the area so that your gentle handle doesn't turn into a "he-said-she-said" confrontation. Stick to the facts, just the facts.

Offer a Complete Solution

What is it that a customer wants from complaining? Most of the time there is a problem, and they want to know that it is going to be fixed. So, if fixing a problem is what the customer wants, make darned certain that the problem is fixed, not just that tempers are assuaged. You can calm a customer with nice words and a sweet apology, but unless the customer leaves feeling fully heard, fairly treated, and that something specific has been done to prevent the problem from reoccurring, you still have an unhappy, dissatisfied customer.

Listen; ask questions; take notes. Summarize your understanding so that there is no doubt that you have the information needed to fix the problem.

Cement the Relationship

Always end the communication by telling the customer exactly what has been done or what and when something will be done. Always thank the customer for helping you uncover a missed opportunity to serve. Don't let a customer leave unhappy.

POS Point: Always follow up on a complaint. Let the customer know what was done and be sure that the fix really worked.

Here is a side point: The customer is not always right. There really are folks who are out to take advantage of you. Don't worry; they'll get theirs. That's why there is hell! Seriously, folks, the customer really isn't always right. When customers want more than they pay for, that's not right. When customers complain just for the sake of attention, that's not right. Pitiful maybe, but definitely not right. And when customers abuse your crew, your internal customers, they are not right. They are wrong! In that case the customer isn't a customer, and you have every right as well as a responsibility to stand up for your crew. Remember, not all business is good business.

POS Point: If doing business with someone results not in a profit but instead, creates a liability in terms of money or morale, you have every right and reason to refuse that business.

When you have dealt fairly with a legitimate complaint, cement the relationship by offering something as part of your apology. Do something extra, something "above and beyond."

Handling complaints requires patience, even the ability to love the most difficult. It's the most difficult person who needs love the most!

Our fax machine started to hum one afternoon. In a matter of seconds, two pages slipped onto the paper tray. It was a copy of a meeting agenda followed by a handwritten note. The agenda announced "Positively Outrageous Service! by . . ." The name that followed was not mine! Nor did it belong to any of our staff POS coaches. The note said simply, "I think your attorney ought to give this person a call." It was signed by one of our clients (and friend; really one and the same when you do business right).

Let me first say that I've got a wonderful support group in our office. I wouldn't trade any of them for any reason. They haven't much tolerance for anyone who would mistreat either me or Melanie. So, our office staff started to buzz. They were incensed that someone would so blatantly steal our material!

"Call the attorney! That will fix 'em!" was the unanimous sentiment.

No. That isn't the way to handle things. What we need is a little old-fashioned Positively Outrageous Service.

I dialed the association for whom the mystery speaker was scheduled to perform and got the number I needed. Within minutes I had the POS impostor on the line and had introduced myself.

"Are you the same T. Scott Gross who wrote *Positively Outrageous Service?*"

"Yes. I'm really proud of that one."

"I guess you are calling about the presentation coming up in Chicago."

"Yes, I was surprised to discover that I was speaking in Chicago. I'm booked on that date and felt better when I saw that you had it covered. Actually, the suggestion around here is that I should have my attorney mention that to you. But, if you've read the book, you won't be surprised that I feel a little differently."

"I guess I should have asked," replied a pretty sheepish voice.

"That would have been the right thing to do. But, so long as you didn't and you seem to have the program covered, have you got a few minutes? I'd like to pass along a few tips that I've learned about POS since writing the book. They might help you give a better presentation."

You could feel the tension drain out of the voice as threat turned to surprise. I shared my thoughts and said that I would be sending a half-dozen autographed books to be given to the audience. Surprise became absolute delight.

"I want you to know something," said the voice.

"Sure! Go right ahead."

"That was really Positively Outrageous Service. I half expected you to sue me. I'll never do that again, I promise!"

And I believe that is so. And I am absolutely certain that I made a friend.

(Now don't read this and think you can get me for a freebie. I may be out of town when the next fax comes in and Mom just isn't going to put up with it!)

Many people hear the story about the unauthorized use of my materials (there have been many instances), and they are surprised at my handling. As my good friend Mark Mayberry says, "Positively Outrageous Service isn't a gimmick. It's a way of life. Some people just aren't going to get it." Amen!

PRESTO, GOOFO!

Cindy Butler CMP, meeting planner extraordinaire, was in a panic when she arrived at 6 A.M. to set up registration for a meeting scheduled to start at 8:30 when, surprise, the room was not set anywhere close to her plan. Convention services' staff were not scheduled to arrive on site until 7:30, making the changeover nearly impossible.

As Cindy was about to, shall we say, make her displeasure known, a houseman calmly walked by and exchanged room names, moving her meeting to another room that was appropriately set!

Well, ya gotta give 'em at least a "C" for creativity!

BUZZ JOB

A sparkle of a POS practitioner, Ann Devers of the National Air Transport Association wrote to tell of Doug McNeely, manager of the Montgomery Airport in Gaithersburg, Maryland.

> An early morning call came from a nearby resident complaining about noise from a particular aircraft that had taken off that morning. Instead of sending his normal "I'm sorry" letter, he decided these people needed a little more attention.
>
> Doug went to their house with an information brochure about the airport, its economic importance to the community, etc., along with a coupon for a Discovery Flight for the couple.
>
> When they arrived at the airport, Doug gave them a grand tour, which included the county's traffic airplane, the county's police helicopter and the CAP planes. Doug then had them go up on the first flight in a small plane. As they flew, Doug pointed out their house and its proximity to the airport and explained why the noise was sometimes greater than at others.
>
> This couple, in turn, spread the information they received from Doug throughout their neighborhood. Calls of complaints have slowed, leaving Doug more time to direct airport expansion!

TALK ABOUT A GUARANTEE!

A customer of Men's Wearhouse writes:

> I purchased a suit several months ago with the understanding that it would travel well. Unfortunately, the material was so soft that after several

hours of normal office wear it was horribly wrinkled. I mentioned this to John, my salesman, on several occasions, and he always offered to press it for free.

Finally, after wearing it on a two-day trip, I came to the conclusion that the suit was not what I thought it was and not what I needed. I brought the suit in to John and, after a brief conversation, he agreed to exchange it. I was so pleased with the whole situation that after I picked out a replacement I bought two more suits!

SELLING COMMANDMENTS FOR SERVICE FANATICS

ugust 1st. In two weeks, Melanie and I will have been married twenty-one years. I suspect there will be another thirty, forty, or more until time at least temporarily, breaks the bond that has made us friends and lovers, partners and collaborators for so long. This morning, floating high over the southwest desert, I leaned over, pulled away the microphone on Melanie's headset, and planted a smooch, just because. Life can be very, very good. And therein lies the secret to every sale, whether it is the sale of a product, a service, or an idea.

Twenty-one years ago I was busy selling a brown-eyed girl on the idea of spending the rest of her life with me. Maybe you've made a similar sales presentation, or maybe you'd like to. Or maybe, sadly, you think you may have attended one too many such sales proposals.

Whenever you have purchased with either money or your time, you did so for one reason and one reason only—you thought that the purchase would bring you happiness. You thought that, as a result of your participation in the transaction, you would feel good.

The promise of feeling good is the only reason people ever buy or buy into anything. Well, there is one other reason. Sometimes we buy not so much to feel good as we do to avoid feeling bad.

Most marketing campaigns are goofy. They only tell you what you should buy. They forgot to tell you how your purchase decision will bring "feel good" to your life.

There are only two approaches to marketing. You can talk about the price, product, packaging, and the place. We call this *awareness marketing*. Or there is an emotional approach, and that is talk about the promise of "feel good," which is called, appropriately enough, *"feel good" marketing*.

Remember, the dark side of the search for feeling good is the rush to avoid feeling bad. Sometimes those two emotions are so close they're nearly indistinguishable.

For example, take the commercials for cellular phones. They started out as a statement of features and benefits. You can call the office for messages or to reschedule an appointment if you are running late. That's strictly awareness marketing: features and benefits piled on others.

But why did I buy my cell phone? Simple. My son told me that his mom needed one for safety. "If she has car trouble on the way to or from San Antonio, she can call for help instead of trusting that someone honest will stop."

Sold! One for each car!

That is the element of "feel good," or maybe the avoidance of feeling bad at its finest.

Even though the concept is simple, there are a jillion ways to take advantage of this principle.

POS Point: Take advantage of your knowledge about human nature and selling but never, never take advantage of the customer!

Following are my "Ten Commandments of Selling," which will make you a sales superstar, while winning the respect and admiration of your customers.

ONE: SELL THE SOLUTION, NOT THE PROBLEM

People don't buy stuff. They buy "feel good."

A garden tractor is not a four-wheeled something to park in the garage. It is a convenient way to a beautiful lawn. In fact, one of our favorite clients, Toro, says that they are in business to promote a beautiful environment. Get it? Feelings instead of stuff.

A restaurant doesn't sell food. It sells the promise that you will enjoy a dining experience of rich tastes and gracious service. Okay, so some restaurants only sell the prospect that you won't be hungry. (See the dictionary listing under "airline food"! Actually, some airline food is pretty good.)

Speaking of food, supermarkets are no longer in the food business. Now they are selling the answer to "What's for dinner?" Grocers are selling meal replacements positioned along the promise of "eat this and you'll feel good," rather than the more traditional approach of "we have corn in every size can imaginable."

Dry cleaners should be selling the promise that you will look great while spending less time, and car dealers should be selling transportation that fits your lifestyle rather than a payment that you can handle.

The smart salespeople sell ideas. The rest sell stuff.

We lunched at an Applebee's and were pleasantly surprised when our server introduced himself as a "table-side marketing specialist." When we asked how that was different from the more expected title of server, he smiled and said, "They bring you food so you won't be hungry. I help you select a meal that will make you smile!"

So who would you want to serve you? A server or a table-side marketing specialist?

When we bought our airplane, the salesman told us all about the avionics and engine, answering all our questions about financing and insurance. But he didn't say much about how we might use the darned thing. He didn't tell me stories about how other people saved time or had great flying experiences. He was selling me an airplane, but I wanted an experience and the convenience of flying! It was a good thing that I was already sold on the concept!

Think of anything that you have ever bought and remember how you felt. Remember what you really wanted out of the transaction. Your first car, your first home, your first date! Did you run around telling everyone about the great deal? And if you mentioned features and benefits, were you really excited about the paint job or was it the feeling driving around in a candy-apple-red car that actually got to you? As for your house or apartment, what was it that really turned you on? I'll bet when you moved in you had a picture of sitting on the balcony at sunset or an idea about how you would landscape the front yard. Feelings—"feel good" feelings—are what people buy. You just have to be smart enough to sell them!

A second most-missed sales opportunity has to be that so few sales people think of selling as a service.

I reread Michael LeBoeuf's terrific book, *How to Win Customers and Keep Them for Life.* He said, "There's a big difference between selling and helping people to buy." How true! You could also put it like this, "There is a big difference between selling stuff and solving problems." Too many salespeople see a customer and think, "I wonder how many bucks this guy has? There must be a way to get them all." Better to see a customer and think, "I wonder what kind of problem this customer is trying to solve. There must be a way that I can be a part of the solution."

What is the difference between those two scenarios? Better, how are those two scenarios similar? In either case, you will end up with all the money that the customer is prepared to spend and maybe a little more. The difference lies only in how the customer feels. If you look for clever approaches to close the sale, serve up transparent marketing gimmicks, and add a little pressure to the situation, even though you may end up with all of the customer's bucks, the customer walks away feeling sold rather than served.

If in your industry you simply have no use for repeat or referral business, then by all means, if you can face yourself in the mirror, have at it. But on the outside chance that you think you might benefit from customers who want to come back or who will be willing to send someone else your way, stick to selling as an opportunity to solve problems, to serve the customer, rather than yourself.

The big opportunity in sales lies in selling more to the customer that you already have than in selling to more customers. The hot issue in sales today is customer share as opposed to market share.

One of the most effective ways to measure the healthiness of an organization is frequency of purchases. In the days of owning a restaurant, we lived and died not on inventory turnover and cash control but on our ability to make a customer feel so good about their decision to eat at our place that they came in again—and soon!

Frequency comes from "feel good." Make the customer feel so good about their purchase decision that they come in more often and tell others. You have one of the keys to profits because now you are spending time loving the customer that you already have rather than looking for another to take the place of the last guest served.

One of the biggest expenses in selling is not making the sale. The biggest expense is getting to that moment where you might make a sale; it is finding and attracting the customer that capture our resources and attention.

In our own business, we pay a huge premium to bureaus to locate and qualify meeting planners who might be interested in our services as keynote speakers and workshop leaders. The best sale we ever make is the one where a longtime customer (who belongs to us and not to a bureau) calls and wants a repeat engagement. Therein lies the profit—selling more to a customer already found.

"You skin this one while I go kill another one" is the mantra of the old days of mass marketing.

Today, there is no mass market.

Just look at television, at the folks who put the mass in media. In the old days, which today applies to any date more than 24 hours' past, marketers would create a product and test it in Peoria. If it played in Peoria, our middle America, it would be deemed a likely consumer hit. This was a great approach in the days when the average grocery store was under 10,000 square feet. Today, grocery stores are often ten times that size.

In 1972 there were 6.2 square feet of retail space per capita in the United States. Twenty years later that number was 18.4, nearly three times more retail space, and no one knows how many more products.

Remember when NBC, ABC, and CBS were about it? Remember when CNN came on the scene and folks were certain that rich Ted Turner was about to become poor Ted Turner? You can laugh now, Ted!

Today, there are so many places to buy and even more vehicles by which to be sold that consumers are into product and choice overload. And worse for the retailer, the customer is ever more difficult to find. When there were three television choices on any given night, you could bet your customer was behind channel number one, channel number two, or channel number three. Today, clicker in hand, your customer is surfing a 150 channels with more on the way! Better to sell more to the customer you have.

The first commandment is key because selling solutions rather than stuff is how you sell more to customers you already have, and solutions almost always require more stuff.

Is the problem a more comfortable living room? The solution is more than a reclining chair. This might take a new television, a table lamp, or even a coat of paint.

Is the problem transportation? The solution could be a new car, insurance, even defensive-driving lessons. Let your imagination be your guide. Whatever you do, dream about solving problems, not selling the stuff. The stuff gets sold as a by-product of problems getting solved!

TWO: PRACTICE RECIPROCITY

I love the word *reciprocity*. It sounds so new-age, so sophisticated.

Reciprocity simply means that if you do something for a customer, in order to feel comfortable with themselves, they are compelled to do something for you—like buy. Maybe buy is too strong a word. How about *listen*? When you love on a customer, the very least that customer will do is listen to your pitch.

The man who gave a name to reciprocity is Robert Cialdini. Cialdini wrote a wonderful (although kind of egg-heady) book: *Influence, the Psychology of Persuasion*. If you are serious about service and selling, you absolutely must read this book.

I learned about reciprocity from Fred Vang. Fred is quite possibly the world's greatest salesman for a number of reasons. First, Fred loves his customers. He always puts them first. Second, Fred loves selling. And third, a very close third in Fred's case, Fred sees selling as an opportunity to serve.

Fred taught me about reciprocity when he told me how he used tea to sell luxury cars. Fred had a customer who was a particularly tough sell. Better to say, a particularly difficult customer.

This customer wanted to nickel-and-dime Fred for every last penny of profit.

Well, Fred recognized that this particular gentleman not only loved tea, but he was a connoisseur of tea. So Fred purchased a selection of the finest teas that he could locate and had them ready when the gentleman visited.

When the gentleman recognized that he was about to lose

his negotiating position by accepting the tea, he at first refused. But when Fred described the exotic choices and admitted that he would be hurt to have his hospitality denied, the
gentleman caved.

In a matter of minutes, the ice was broken; and, in short
order, Fred had an order for an expensive automobile at a fair
price and an equally fair profit.

A few months later the gentleman found himself in need
of yet another automobile and, naturally, he called Fred. Only
this time he made an appointment on the condition that Fred
would not serve tea!

Fred had the highest closing ratio at the dealership in
large part because of his recognition of the power of reciprocity. He would take some customers across the street to a juice
bar where, over friendly conversation and a glass of cold juice,
Fred would close deal after deal.

Reciprocity. Do a little something for me, make me feel
good by putting me first, and I will do for you.

In Dallas there is a wonderful store called Cowtown
Boots. I needed boots but didn't want to spend the bucks.
Melanie insisted that we stop at Cowtown. After all, we were
in Dallas, and if anyone would have boots to fit my long,
skinny feet, it would be them.

"Okay. We can look. But I'm not going to buy. Let's get
out of the heat," I finally agreed.

Two steps into the store, we were greeted by a Texas drawl
that bellowed out from beneath the broad brim of a black
cowboy hat. Whoever this was, he was all hat and boots. Not
much of his face escaped that outfit save a rather crooked
smile.

"Hot out there, isn't it?"

"You've got that right."

"How about a cold beer?"

"You've got cold beer?"

"Name it and it's yours, partner!"

"Well, if it's cold, anything light will be just fine. Do you have those Dan Post boots that look kinda well-worn already?"

"Sure do! And I've got a dollar that says we have your size whatever it is!"

In a matter of minutes I was trompin' around the store, steppin' high, admiring the boots, and sipping a cold beer. You know that on a hot day the best part of a cold beer is the first sip. So I took the first sip, tromped a little more, came back for another "first sip," and then went back to the trompin'.

I bought the boots.

Reciprocity.

And reciprocity works just fine when you are the customer.

When we bought our office furniture, I was a little overwhelmed by the price tag. It was one of those "suck-cold-air-through-your-teeth" moments. The kind of moment when you ask yourself dumb questions like, "What's money if it isn't to spend?", right before you spend more than you should.

Before I signed on the dotted line, I asked Melanie if we could walk down the street for a bite of lunch. Sort of a last meal before we would be too poor to afford food again in this lifetime.

We had lunch and talked about how this was the perfect furniture and how maybe we would win the lottery.

On the way out, I asked Melanie to buy free delivery when she paid the check. "Free delivery?" she asked.

"Or something close to it. Pick out a real nice selection of cookies and muffins. I remember them saying at the store that they have been so busy that no one had taken lunch. Pick out something nice."

Now, I'd like to think that Melanie and I are nice people to begin with. Hey, we do have a policy that anyone who is at our house during a meal period eats! That applies to contractors and employees, customers and kids. If you're there and we have food, you eat. For us sharing food has always been a reward in itself. But this time I thought it might have a greater value.

We delivered the goodies, passing them around the store, even dragging in a few customers as we joked that we were about to sign our lives away over a desk and a few odd pieces of wood.

"You know," I said to Jeff, the owner, as I picked up the pen. "This is a really big-ticket. I just can't feel good about paying this much money for furniture and having to pay another 300 bucks for delivery." I paused.

Jeff smiled, "This is the muffins, isn't it?"

"Something like that," I smiled, wishing that I had a cup of Fred's tea to celebrate the moment.

Good salespeople, whether they are selling a customer on a product or selling a salesperson on lowering the price or otherwise sweetening the deal, practice reciprocity.

When we first coined the term *Positively Outrageous Service,* we knew that there was incredible power in the idea of pleasantly surprising the customer. Now we can say that Positively Outrageous Service works just as well on either side of the transaction. Surprise the server before the transaction and you create the tension that is reciprocity. But surprise the customer after the sale, and again, you create a tension toward reciprocity.

Have you ever been given a business card and not had one to give in return? The tension of reciprocity. The secret is that little things create the most powerful tension. Give someone something big and you create anger or distrust. Give something big for little or no reason and it's obvious that you have offered a bribe.

Sometimes even small gifts arouse suspicion. Try walking down the street putting coins in parking meters and see what happens. Some will think you are a saint. Others will just call you nuts. But many will confront you saying, "Just what do you think you are doing?" (I've heard that in some cities, putting coins in the meter in front of a stranger's car is actually illegal!)

Be careful! Reciprocity can backfire! The Scientologists have a word for reciprocity gone too far. They call it "out exchange." When you are "out exchange," one of the parties has given far more than the other, creating ill feelings, not in the one who gave but in the one who was unable to give proportionately.

You've known people who want to be martyrs. "Don't worry about me. Let me do this for you," they whine as they give and give and make you painfully aware of their sacrifice. Do you feel more love for them? No! Being "out exchange" makes you angry! So be careful to play reciprocity to the finish. And the finish is always allowing your customer, or partner, to reciprocate by doing something for you, like buying or telling someone about your wonderful product or service, or giving you the name of another potential customer.

Vacuum cleaner salespeople have recognized reciprocity for years. One salesperson I know loved to have customers treat him rudely. These, he said, were the ones most likely to give him a referral since his gracious handling of their lack of manners instilled a need to make amends by giving him a list of their friends more likely to buy.

The secret to creating reciprocity is to give some thing or some service that is of just the right size. Not too big, not too small, but juuuusssst . . . right!

After the sale is often the very best time to create reciprocity. Send a small gift, write a simple thank-you card, or call to see if the product or service has met the customer's needs and you create a final sweet impression that transcends the other part of the deal.

At our restaurant we used to call folks to whom we had delivered that day to ask how everything was. That created reciprocity tension of the simplest kind. Customers would tell their friends that we had taken the time to inquire about a four-dollar delivery order. "Incredible service," they would say as they relieved their reciprocity tension by telling someone how nice we were!

Perhaps the best form of reciprocity creation is described by the Cajuns as *lagniappe,* which means "a little something extra." Say you negotiate a big deal, or even a little one for that matter. You have carefully agreed on price and product. But when you deliver, you deliver a little something extra. That creates reciprocity tension of the best kind.

Two wheeler-dealers negotiate to the last nickel, but the winner will be the one who delivers as promised and then throws in something totally unexpected. That turns heads, but most importantly, it moves tongues and creates a tension for reciprocity that far exceeds the original deed when it's time to deal again. Reciprocity creates greater value for the giver than for the receiver.

Look for little ways to exceed your agreement.

Reciprocity has one other important feature. It is the smallest part of the transaction, but it is the most memorable—and talked about—part of the deal. You bought a $200,000 house with features and benefits out the wazoo and what do you talk about? The funny soap dish the realtor gave you for the bathroom.

I was looking for a perfect example to give here and couldn't think of one to save my soul. When I looked through my notes, I realized I was holding one!

A few months ago I spoke to the National Art Materials Trade Association and met an interesting couple who had an even more interesting product. It's a refillable notebook, really cool, with paper refills and a neat cover that looks like it will last forever. I really wanted one when I saw it at the trade show. But this show, like most, did not allow retail sales, so I drooled and decided to purchase one at the first opportunity.

When I called the association for another reason, I decided on a whim to ask for the phone number of the folks at Inspiral. I then called to ask for a list of retailers who sold their products when the owner picked up the phone.

"Are you the guy we met in Toronto? The speaker who talked about Positively Outrageous Service?"

"That's me! I love your notebooks and just have to find out who sells them so I can get one."

"Well, you gave us such a wonderful mention in your talk, I've been wanting to send you one just to say thanks!"

That's reciprocity all right.

I really go out of my way to keep folks from giving me special treatment just for doing my job, but Mike insisted and I gave in.

Now I owned everything I could possibly want, except apparently, an Inspiral notebook. It's the darndest thing, but for days I would volunteer to walk out for the mail hoping that my notebook would be waiting. In about a week, there it was. I opened the package and beamed like a two-year-old at Christmas. My notebook, complete with an extra refill! I was thrilled.

And now I have to tell everyone about it.

As Yogi Berra would say, "Reciprocity all over again!"

THREE: GET IT RIGHT

The one thing that will bring customers in again and again is the security of knowing that no matter what, you are on their side; that no matter what, if things go wrong, you will make them right.

I met one of our customers while shopping in the city.

"Hi! I don't know the name but the face is familiar. I'm Scott Gross. I own the Church's Chicken, and I know you are one of my customers."

"Sure am! I really like eating at your place."

I got all puffed up ready to reel in the compliments that I knew were soon to follow.

"Is it the food?" I was sure of the answer.

"It's okay," he replied, as my chest began to fall.

"Well, I guess it must be our new dining room?"

"Nice, but nothin' to write home about."

"Well, what is it? The friendly service?"

"Actually, sometimes you guys really screw things up . . ."

"And you like that?" I interrupted. "Are you wearing leather somewhere I can't see?"

"No. It's just over the years I've seen you guys really get things messed up. You know, wrong order and such. And it's not that I really want to get the wrong order, but boy, I've never been anywhere where they go to such lengths to make things right. We don't exactly hope things go wrong, but we know that if they do, your crew will be like white on rice trying to set things straight!"

The next best thing to getting what you want, when you want it, and the way you want it is being absolutely positive that, if things aren't right the first time, someone will make absolutely certain that they will be made right—and then some!

In the previous chapter, we stated that service-minded organizations have a policy that goes something like this: When things go wrong for whatever reason, they will be made right, no questions asked.

We also said that customers who have never had a reason to complain are not as loyal as customers who have had a complaint that was successfully resolved. A customer that you have been serving for years, with never a problem, or never a reason to question your service or product integrity, is not as loyal as a customer with whom you have had at least one service "oops."

If you think about it, it makes perfectly good sense.

A corollary to this rule might be: Apologize even when the customer is unaware that you goofed. Now think about it. This idea can give you the best of both worlds. A customer who has had consistently good product and service will now feel that your commitment to put him first has been tested. Result? A loyal customer.

The best example I have ever heard comes from a friend

who dined at Red Lobster. At the time they were running a lunch special that promised lunch served in ten minutes or less or you eat free. My friend ordered lunch; it came quickly and everything seemed just perfect when the manager appeared at the table.

"I apologize for the delay in preparing your lunch. It's on the house today with my compliments. Please give us another try real soon."

My friend's jaw went slack. The service had been fast and friendly, the lunch hot and delicious, certainly no need for an apology and definitely no reason to comp the meal. What's your guess as to this customer's loyalty as well as the probability that I am not by any measure the only person that he told?

Another good friend took her son to Chevy's in Denver. (This was one of those mother-son bonding events, just a little one-on-one time between parent and teenage child.) Service time must have taken too long to suit the folks at Chevy's, even though our friend and her son were deep into conversation and really enjoying themselves when the manager appeared at their table with guest check and apology in hand. Again, an apology without a noticeable cause, but definitely a loyalty-building move.

Smart operators jump on problems like "white on rice." Smarter operators don't wait for the customer to notice the problem. The smartest operators make a show out of opportunities to set things straight as this builds loyalty among customers who notice the show, but who were otherwise uninvolved.

FOUR: PRACTICE EXCLUSIVITY

Desirability, believability, convenience, and exclusivity are four factors that influence the customer's perception of value. Is it something I want or need? Does this offer look like it's actually deliverable? Have they made buying easy? Is it really something special?

Desirability—you've got that one.

Believability—this is simple. Is this offer too good to be true? Has the offer been presented in such a way that I doubt your integrity? For example, we watched a news report on ticket scalping. One of the most interesting segments involved a well-dressed executive attempting to give away four box-seat tickets to a big game. This guy could hardly get people to talk to him. Four box-seat tickets and you want to give them away? Must be something wrong with that! No way, pal!

There may always be a situation where creating a reason to buy now makes sense, but for the most part consumers are pretty savvy. They know when they are being conned. The terminally goofy may buy, but the big money stays home because they detest being conned and manipulated.

I see speakers pushing product from the platform and making big bucks. I also see speakers pushing ideas from the platform and making bigger bucks.

A favorite example is the "show special." Is there anyone on the planet who does not understand that if you ask for the show's special prices—even months after the show—that you can get them? There's always a special price just for the asking. So ask if you are the customer and stop the blatant manipulation if you are the seller.

Convenience is factor number three. Have you made it easy to buy? This could be anything from arranging payments that I can afford, a favorite tactic in automobile sales, to something as simple as providing a bag to carry my purchase in.

The car people understand the idea of convenience in a big way. Smart, although I am not sure about ethical, car salespeople sell a customer on a payment, rather than the price of the car. The rubes are led willingly to the cleaners.

"Would you like to drive this car home today if I can get you a payment of $250?"

Say "yes" to that one and you'll get the car, all right. But before you accept the keys, try writing a check with your nose. You may as well, you'll be paying through it!

I didn't say that this was right. It's just an example of making it easy for the customer to purchase.

How about something as simple as providing a bag to carry the purchase in? We were wandering through an arts and crafts fair in the Hill Country when we spotted a ceramic container that would be perfect for the kitchen. No, too heavy to carry, until the sharp artist-entrepreneur offered a plastic bag. She even suggested that she could hold our prior purchase, too. Sold. The product that minutes before had been too heavy was now conveniently packaged and held for us to pick up on the way out.

Convenience is a major issue in buying decisions.

When we had our restaurant, we asked and received permission from our franchisor to add chicken tenders to the menu. Through creative sampling of a really wonderful product, we were able to take chicken tenders to an astounding 24 percent of sales.

Four years later, the franchisor noticed that we were hitting a home run with this product. (Duh!) They asked us to provide instructions in great detail, which we gladly did. For thirteen weeks, they called us every Monday for a sales report on the product, with more questions about cooking times, packaging, and marketing.

Then they discovered that we were doing it completely wrong!

When the company rolled out their version of the product, it was packaged on a large paper plate covered with a clear plastic dome when served to go. It was a beautiful but difficult presentation. Our tenders were served over a bed of Cajun fries with a side of country-style pepper gravy for dipping in our regular chicken box. Our customers would pull into our drive-through, pick up an order of tenders, pop open the box, and enjoy the tenders and fries as finger food while they were running errands or driving to their next appointment.

Tenders packaged on the plate looked good, but they immediately became part of the upholstery when you pulled the dome off while driving. Company sales immediately climbed to a whopping 6 percent, then fell slowly from there. Our sales of the product, which we were preparing completely wrong, remained at 24 percent!

Were we just lucky or was there something about the convenience of our product that made a difference?

Now the biggie: Exclusivity.

Today there is an incredible trend toward polarized buying habits. Consumers have discovered that there are some products for which there is no useful service component. These are commodity products, and consumers almost always make their buying decisions based solely on price and convenience. If you are selling a commodity product, even a commodity service, you had better have the lowest price in town. If you don't, take your highlighting pen and make a few whacks across this page. When a product is exclusive, you can sell it at a higher price. If you can find it on any street corner, price becomes the overriding issue.

Take a look at the burger business. There is a hamburger joint everywhere you look. Even my friends at burger powerhouse McDonald's describe the market as "hostile." They recognize that when you can get a quality burger everywhere, price becomes the overriding issue.

And out of that comes the $.99 burger wars and Taco Bell with their "value pricing" strategy. Price becomes the issue when products become commodities. Exclusivity allows you to charge—and get—a higher price than possible for a similar but less exclusive product.

Why do you think the major leagues and the Olympic Commission make a big deal out of licensing products? Because if anyone could legally use their logo, manufacturers could not command a premium price for logo products. People will pay more for one-of-a-kind or few-of-a-kind products. They're exclusive.

We once watched an Olympic sidebar story on pin collecting. It seemed that everybody in and out of Atlanta, Georgia, had the bug. The Varsity Diner, a hamburger joint turned Atlanta landmark, issued a pin of their own. Brilliant marketing, I thought. One problem, though. The Varsity was rather famous for its onion rings, so the rings were a featured part of the pin design. The Olympic Commission took one look at the pin, determined that the five onion rings on the pin looked suspiciously like the trademarked Olympic rings, and cried foul, or attorney, or whatever you cry in situations like this.

The Varsity had to send the pins back to the manufacturer to be reworked. One hundred of the pins had already been sold or given away. Do you have any idea what those one hundred pins are worth? How about $250? And this for the pin of an Atlanta greasy spoon!

Exclusivity puts points on the board and bucks in your pocket. What could you do to make your product more exclusive?

Our Mooney airplane is Mooney niner five mike kilo. That's the call sign that we use to identify ourselves on the radio. It is also the tail number, which is painted on both sides: 95MK. The 95 indicates that our Mooney was built in 1995; the M stands for Mooney; and the K is the substitute for 10,000. Pilots in the know see our Mooney and realize in a heartbeat that this is the ten-thousandth Mooney ever built and that we are flying a one-of-a-kind commemorative edition. It has a distinctive paint job that the folks at Mooney say is reserved exclusively for my airplane. I would have paid extra for that. Heck, I probably did!

FIVE: ATTRACT CUSTOMERS

Good servers and salespeople do not wait for customers to come to them. They go in search of opportunities to serve. So I am not about to tell you to sit back and passively wait until a customer comes your way. What I am going to tell you is that the truly great have to prospect less because they are careful to keep the customers that they already have.

While in Phoenix we had dinner with Elke and Michael LeBoeuf. Michael wrote the wonderful book I mentioned earlier, *How to Win Customers and Keep Them for Life*. Notice that he doesn't focus solely on finding new customers. He says that finding is only half of the issue; keeping them is the hard part.

And how do you keep customers?

First, you have to know what it is that customers are buying. Surprise, a lot of the attraction is you!

Ya gotta have personality! That's what customers buy. It's included, like it or not, in the purchase price.

Every store, office, or plant has a distinctive personality. Part of what franchising attempts to do is to create a personality that customers love, standardizing it through decor and procedure. Too bad. A nice idea that doesn't work.

The most highly standardized operations in the world are Marriott and McDonald's. And any "road warrior" and any four-year-old can tell you that in spite of all the standardization, no two are anywhere near being exact copies of another. Why? Because most of an operation's personality comes from the people who run it. You cannot train people to smile any more than you can command them to be happy.

THE PERSONALITY DRAIN

One of the biggest crocks perpetuated on the service sector of the economy is the idea of TQM. Total Quality Management is exactly what you do not want in a service business.

The point of TQM is the elimination of variance, a noble and worthy idea especially in a manufacturing environment where you can use your statistical process control to measure and count until you turn blue. But in hospitality (and what business is not hospitality?) you want variance. In service business, variance is good!

Why? Because every customer is different! No two of us are exactly alike. We all want something just a little different from the other guy. (Unless you are a teenager. This special, God-love'em group is exempt from this discussion as most have not yet achieved full humanhood.)

The instant that you begin insisting that every customer be greeted and treated alike is the instant to recognize that you are out of the people business.

Allowing and encouraging employees to bring their personalities to the sales and service process introduces the possibility that your business will develop an attractive personality that will attract customers and cause them to stay.

We took a writing break to exercise and dip in the hotel pool where we met Jennette and Carl from La Jolla. Jennette said she was involved in "high-end retailing of gently worn designer clothing." (For those who are culturally slow, she said that she sells expensive used clothes. Got it?)

Jennette used to sell at traditional boutiques but has since gone into the "gently worn" segment of the industry. From selling extremely expensive clothes to women with too much time and money, she now sells very expensive used clothing to women with too much time and not quite so much money. She told us that, much to her surprise, most of her customers had followed her to her new calling.

Why be surprised? They were never buying from a particular store as much as they were buying from Jennette.

Haven't you noticed that when hairstylists change salons, within a week the customer base turns over as well? Why would you think that any business would be all that different?

When a car salesperson moves, so does the customer base. This is true for waitresses and waiters and practically anywhere customers have an easy choice.

The principle holds for places where the choice is not quite so simple. Customers choose where they shop based on the personality of the store. And the personality of the store is nothing more than the combined personality of the people who work there tempered by the way they are managed.

We like to reminisce about the good old days of ma-and-pa businesses. Anyone who grew up in the 1950s and 1960s has a fond memory of a corner store run by a sweet old couple, that is, the kind of folks who would slip you a piece of penny candy or let you come back later to pay for the milk if you came up a little short in cash.

What we don't recall are the stores run by little old couples who would cut your heart out for leaning on the counter glass. Think hard and you will realize that just because a business is a ma-and-pa business, there is no guarantee that the service will be warm and friendly.

POS Point: Every business is a ma-and-pa business.

Even the big-box discounters are ma-and-pa businesses. Somebody's ma or somebody's pa is in charge. And they may be as sweet as the old couple who ran the corner store in your neighborhood. They could also be mean as snakes. Whatever the case, their personality is the personality of the store or business.

POS Point: The biggest issue in all of business is not quality, it's not price. It's personality.

What kind of personality does your shop have? When customers do business with you, do they feel all warm and tingly inside? Do they feel like trusted and respected members of the family? Or are they ignored by the help and insulted by your policies? The personality of your business attracts and keeps customers.

SIX: BE A QUALITY FANATIC

Or hire my wife! Fortunately for you, Melanie is hot on the trail of errors and goofs in this book. She won't let this book go anywhere until it has her seal of approval. Every business needs a Melanie, someone who will not rest until everything is perfect. Better yet, we all need to be Melanies, relentless seekers of detailed perfection.

Al DiLiberto walked into the kitchen of his restaurant, Boccone's, and noticed immediately that something didn't smell just the way it was supposed to smell. Instead of the lure of fresh-baked bread, Al, who has a nose like a bloodhound (we're talking ability not size), noticed that something smelled, well, sort of burnt.

"What's going on with the bread?"

"We sorta overcooked it."

"Why is it on the rack and not in the trash?"

"There's a lot of it."

"So?"

"It's almost time for dinner."

"So toss it! We can afford to dump the bread. We can't afford to lose our customers!"

Quality f-a-n-a-t-i-c.

If you want to attract customers and keep them forever, you must become a quality fanatic. Not interested in quality. Not concerned about quality. A quality f-a-n-a-t-i-c! Period.

SEVEN: SAY YES!

Look for ways to say "yes" to your customers. In fact, you should have a policy that says only someone in management can tell a customer "no." In the service business, and we're all in the service business, our job is to say "yes" to the customer. The answer is "yes." What's the question?

We arrived at our hotel early. We realized that check-in is not at 10:30 A.M., the time we arrived. So we approached the desk fully expecting to wait. No problem, we'll eat breakfast or lunch or whatever they'll serve us. We expected to wait until a room was available.

The manager at the desk handled our check-in, gave us a

guest ID card, and invited us to return after we had eaten to pick up a room key.

We took our sweet time, enjoying the pleasant surroundings and each other, talking about our latest project. About noon we returned to the front desk, knowing from experience that by noon at least a few rooms are ready.

"Checkout is at ten o'clock, check-in is at four o'clock," said the shift supervisor in a monotone voice that didn't belong to Mr. Happy. Looking at his keyboard, he continued, "Come back at four o'clock."

"Excuse me. Did you say four o'clock?"

"Checkout time is ten o'clock. Check-in time is four o'clock. Come back at four o'clock, and we'll have a room for you."

"I'm sorry. You don't understand. I have no car and no place to go until four o'clock. I came here to write. Do you think you might have a room ready before four o'clock? Surely there will be something ready sooner?"

"You can go the restaurant or the bar. There is an exercise facility where you can change and go to the pool. The bellman will store your luggage. We'll have a room at four o'clock."

I am so proud I did not kill the . . .

Get it? We are all in the hospitality business. I don't care if you run a bank or an auto repair shop or if you dig ditches for a living, you are in the hospitality business. And no business can afford to have someone meet the public who does not have the basic understanding that saying "yes" to customers is how we pay the bills!

(P.S. I got a room. Immediately. It was wonderful. No firearms were involved.)

EIGHT: MAINTAIN PRICE INTEGRITY

I'll never forget the day it happened. We had just completed a large catering order, three hundred pieces of hot, fresh, fried chicken and a mountain of honey-butter biscuits, when the after-church crowd hit us with a vengeance. In restaurant talk, we were getting "slammed."

Christian was working the walk-up counter and, because we were running at full tilt due to the catering order, was just a bit behind on filling orders. He had well over one hundred dollars in carryout orders written on the order board. We all stood waiting, tongs in hand, for the cook's computer to signal that the next batch of bird was ready when an unfamiliar-looking character walked up to the counter and said, "Do ya'll have that $4.99 special I seen on TV in San Antonio?"

"Yes, sir. We do. How many would you like?"

The fellow went on a fishing expedition in his jeans' pocket and hauled out a ten dollar bill that was older and dirtier than the jeans.

"One. And a big cup of ice water. Lots of ice. And a straw. And lots of catsup," he said grabbing a large handful of napkins large enough to wash his pickup truck.

One by one, while the seconds ticked off on the fryer timer, the other waiting customers asked about the $4.99 special. By the time the chicken was up, over one hundred dollars in Sunday morning orders had evaporated, leaving only six $4.99 hardly-any-profit orders on the board.

In a matter of seconds, we had turned a fair profit into a giveaway.

Smart operators stay out of the discount business. Anybody can give it away. It takes brains to sell it! I don't know who said that, but he or she is a retailing genius. Now I'm going to tell you how to do it!

The big issue is price integrity. The instant you start giving away your product (and that can include service) you are telling your customers that your regular price is too high. In fact, customers who see you routinely give away your product or offer extremely deep discounts will feel embarrassed to routinely pay full fare while the first-time buyers, often just bargain-shopping-bottom-feeders, walk off with the best deals.

Discounting unnecessarily hurts even worse.

We had a huge sign posted on our walk-up window at the restaurant. It announced a highly discounted lunch special, a whopping $2.22. One of our regular customers was spotted heading our way. We could see the smoke from his bomb of a pickup truck. By the time he made it to the window, we had his "usual" already packaged and ready to go. He always paid with a five dollar bill, so we even had the proper change in hand.

Funny thing about regular customers. Quite a few of them order the same thing day in and day out. Even though the order never seems to change, they still feel obligated to look over the menu. Maybe they want to be sure that you haven't changed into a Chinese restaurant since the last time they visited!

On this particular day, our regular guy did his regular thing. Only this time, he couldn't quite see the menu due to the huge window banner announcing the "el cheapo" lunch special. No problem, we knew he would come to his senses and order the "usual" which totaled exactly $4.85. We had the 15 cents change in hand.

"Oh, heck!" he said, a bit frustrated that he couldn't see (but surely he knew it). "Just give me one of those."

He was pointing to the $2.22 special.

Now I'm slow. I admit it. But even I knew that there was something wrong with this picture. Let me see. Regular customer, always spends the better part of a five. Now he's still a regular customer, only he wants to spend about half of the usual, and we encouraged him to do it! AHHHHHH!

POS Point: If the price reflects the value, there is no reason to discount. If it does not, lower it!

We are often approached by meeting planners who apologize for having a limited budget, immediately rushing to tell us that speaking to their group would be a wonderful opportunity for "exposure."

Are you aware that you die from overexposure?

Here's the deal: How would you like to be a meeting planner who paid full fee and discover that some other group got the same speaker for half the price?

Al DiLiberto, mentioned earlier, runs a commercial that asks, "Have you ever been out to dinner and noticed that the couple at the next table are using a coupon to eat for half price? Who do you think is paying for that? You are!"

Al goes on to tell why at Boccone's Restaurant you don't get coupons, just great food where everybody pays the same. Smart guy, that Al!

First point of business: Discount to encourage trial if you must, but do it away from your regular customers.

Discount to encourage trial if you must, but never discount your signature product. Discount to encourage trial if you must, but always have an explanation for your regular customers that is at least plausible.

Discount to encourage trial if you must, but never do it on a predictable basis. Otherwise, your customers will learn quickly to wait until the next sale period.

Discount to encourage trial if you must, but never offer a substandard product intended to drive sales as this hurts your reputation for quality far more than it temporarily helps the top line.

All marketing should have getting trial customers as its primary goal.

NINE: ESTABLISH LONG-TERM RELATIONSHIPS

If ever a sales topic was hot, now is the time for relationship selling. There are several ways to look at relationship selling. First, what can you do to establish a long-term relationship with your customers? And second, how can you use that knowledge to sell to your customer the way he or she likes to be sold?

Why establish a long-term relationship with customers? It's more profitable. If you are in the business to serve, relationships allow you to serve better, which makes you more valuable. And that in turn allows you to get paid. Profits or fun, it doesn't matter. Long-term customer relationships should be your goal.

We love new customers, but learning about new customers, while interesting, takes more time than staying current with established customers. When customers pay for expertise (isn't that what customer service is?), they want to deal with the experts. It's tough to be expert in many fields. Better to establish yourself as the guru in one field than jack-of-all trades, master of you-know-what.

It's also cheaper to sell more to customers that you already have than it is to find another customer. Smart operators look for ways to know their customers, to be ready with fresh solutions to new problems as they crop up.

For the last jillion years, consultants have been trying to sell us on the idea of personality styles. It doesn't matter which set of names you choose. What is important is that you recognize that not every customer is alike. And since we are all different, it stands to reason that the same sales approach won't fit us all.

Some want the best price; some want fast service. Some don't care what it costs so long as they are first on their block to have one. Still others need to be romanced into a purchase decision and reassured at every step that their choice is the best. For these folks, buying technology is the toughest purchase. The stuff is obsolete by the time they make up their mind!

This isn't the place to learn about personality styles other than to remind you that we all like to be sold in a manner that is unique to ourselves, changing moment to moment depending on what we are buying and the circumstances surrounding the purchase. For now just get that establishing long-term customer relations is important in that it gives you a chance to pay attention to the way each customer prefers to buy and to tailor both approach and product to their personality.

TEN: BE PERSISTENT

Being persistent is not the same as being obnoxious or applying high pressure. Instead, please recognize that many customers are psychologically incapable of saying "yes" on the first contact, even to an offer that is perfect in every way.

It may seem obvious that we are not talking about restaurants and retailing. Not so. Many people cannot or will not try a new place on one hearing.

Whatever the product or service, multiple impressions yield progressively greater results.

Less than 5 percent of our sales are made on the first call. In fact, our median number is 8.05 calls, or impressions, before qualified buyers say "yes." Which means that if we gave up after the first call, our sales would decline by 95 percent. Half of our sales come after the eighth impression.

Persistence pays.

For more T. Scott Gross . . . www.tscottgross.com

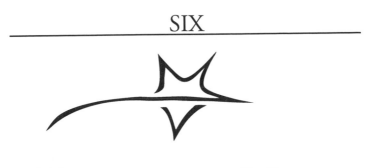

SIX

TRENDS AND MORE

You don't need the history, just the facts. And the fact is we've entered yet another age in the progress of mankind.

We are about to enter the Age of Artistry. Not the Age of Knowledge, which could be defined as data put to work. The Age of Artistry reads as data put to work in creative, innovative ways—and the era is upon us.

And the world knows that I am right. Read the computer magazines and catalogs and you will see the emergence of a huge category of programs that could easily be labeled as "art in a box."

The ham-fisted of the world have recognized that having pure information is no advantage without the ability to put it to work in a manner that surprises and delights.

You can't put art in a box or can. Go to any conference or seminar, walk the halls, peek into the meeting rooms, and what will you see? Thousands of people being held captive in darkened rooms while presenters use state-of-the-art programs and hardware to more efficiently bore them until they are nearly dead.

This is the Age of Artistry when value will derive from information creatively presented. The storyteller will return again to sit with us around the electronic campfire. Mr. Whipple will unwrap the Charmin and invite you to squeeze. And maybe this will bring us a new form of community as technology now denies anonymity.

John Naisbitt nailed it in his book *MegaTrends*. Of course, we're talking about a book that is now old enough to be considered a classic. Classic or not, Naisbitt was clearly ahead of his time when he said that humans crave a high-touch balance to their high-tech world.

Humans can stand just so much high technology before they are psychologically compelled, or driven, to seek balance with high touch. And that is the heart of Positively Outrageous Service.

Think about customer service in terms of human values and you will see that, in large part, the supposed demise of gracious service is the result of service systems that encourage anonymity. The drive-through fast-food joint, bank, credit union, dry cleaner, and mortuary have taught us to deal with one another through a metal-sounding speaker. No face or name, only the tick, tick, tick of someone's franchise service representative clocking the speed of service with a stopwatch in an attempt to get service time to less than a nanosecond.

We drive away served, but not satisfied. Served fast, but not well.

There is little wrong with customer service in this country, or elsewhere, that could not be cured if we denied anonymity. Once servers are allowed to hide behind numbers, once customers are other than neighbors that we know and expect to see again, service goes to hell in the name of speed, turnover, and incremental sales. "Would you like cheese . . . ? No . . . ? Next!"

SERVICE? I DON'T WANT IT!

It's interesting to notice that service quality is in large part determined by our expectations. How a customer feels about the service experience seems to be determined by what they have come to expect of any given service situation. Customers have learned to separate the products and services they buy from the system that delivers them.

Customers have learned that for some products there is no useful service component. Those products they want to buy quick and cheap. Look at the incredible increase in the number of big-box discounters and warehouse stores. Notice that they sell products for which there is little service component. You know how to buy and use dish detergent, vacuum cleaners, and paper plates. They sell 'em bulk and they sell 'em cheap. But I dare you to try and find a salesperson to answer a question or advise you on the purchase.

Even computers are being sold by the discounters. Who is doing the buying? For the most part, first-time buyers of serious computers don't go to the discounters to purchase, or if they do, they don't go alone. But hey! There are fifty million or so computers in the United States these days, so even computers are commodities. You probably use one at work and for certain you know a high school student whom you can drag along to help with your decision.

So what's left to sell after the discounters have run the rest of the retailing world into bankruptcy? Service! That's what!

Service in the new economy, in the Age of Artistry, will have to be truly special. Just as computers have forced us to create more and more involving teaching tools, so will it be that customer service must increasingly engage the customer's imagination. Service, let's call it Positively Outrageous Service, must suck the customer in and make them part of the experience. Indeed, if there is a single watchword for service in these new times, it is "experience."

POS Point: For customer service to ring the bell today, it must invite the customer to be a part of the action. We must wrap an experi-

ence around the transaction. Otherwise the customer will recognize that this product or service needs to be discounted.

POLARIZED BUYING HABITS

Speaking of discounting, customers are not going to tolerate huge premiums for so-so service. In the seventies and eighties, the customer learned that the difference between the retail purchase price and the cost of ingredients to prepare the product at home is the "cost of convenience." This same concept applies to services purchased in the nineties. Only today, service applies to nearly everything.

Take, for example, entertainment. Today we can install, right in our home, entertainment centers that rival the audio and visual clarity of the movie theaters. Give me an experience of long lines, sticky floors and stale popcorn and I'll stay home.

Staying at home is, in itself, a major trend. Not just because Faith Popcorn decided that cocooning was a term in need of coining, but because reality says people are taking at-home time seriously.

A survey by the Wirthlin Group and reported in *The Wall Street Journal* found that 40 percent of the surveyed adults reported that they would be more likely to spend vacation at home than reported just five years ago. Among DINKs (double income, no kids) that number was 60 percent. Plenty of folks are more than willing to take what little time they have and retreat behind locked doors.

Thanks to wonderful and more affordable technology, staying at home is increasingly becoming the experience we used to be able to find only on an expensive night on the town.

Staying at home has become a serious source of competition.

How about shopping? Make it difficult to park, impossible to find a salesperson, inconvenient to schedule a stop, and I'll call Lands' End from my easy chair at eleven o'clock while watching *The Tonight Show*. Besides, they know my size, so there's no need to step into a dressing room.

Name the product—food, entertainment, clothing, power equipment, whatever and I'll show you a product that needs to have an experience wrapped around the purchase transaction.

Today we are seeing polarized buying habits. On one extreme, customers are shouting price, price, price! On the other extreme, they are saying, by their willingness to pay for it, "Give me an experience." Not too many years ago where you shopped was an expression of ability to pay. That is no longer true. You'll find plenty of luxury automobiles parked in front of discount and secondhand stores. Today, bringing home a bargain is more important than nabbing an exclusive brand or label.

What we are seeing is a public that is more and more aware of the difference between the products they want and the service system that delivers those products.

POS Point: When service doesn't count, price is the issue.

SMARTER CONSUMERS

As consumers get smarter, the one thing that retailers cannot afford to discount is the consumer! Consumers know that price and value are not the same thing. They've caught on. They know how much "room" is in any deal. If you intend to sell service, that too will have to be delivered at a value.

The winners in the new economy will be those operators who (1) offer the right combination of intrinsic value and add-on value, (2) give customers service and, therefore, price options, and (3) offer service at a competitive price. We must provide high levels of service efficiently!

At the same time that customers' buying habits are polarizing, so is their ability to pay. In 1970, the average American brought home $298 per week says *Time* (1982 dollars). By 1990, adjusted for inflation, that number had fallen to $257 per week. Tell me that doesn't make a huge difference in the way we spend!

Median family income in 1970 was $35,407 in 1994 dollars (again, *Time*). Today the figure is little changed in spite of the fact that the percentage of the population graduating from a four-year college has doubled. Today 62 percent of married women with children are working. Compare this with only 30 percent 20 years earlier.

A new home purchased in 1970 tipped the mortgage at roughly twice the household's annual earnings. Today that percentage has doubled to 393 percent of annual earnings to pay for the average new home. The difference has to come from somewhere. It's coming in the form of increased consumer buying and customers who have turned bargain hunting and price negotiating into an art form.

Much to my surprise, recent studies indicate that new car buyers actually prefer haggling with the dealerships rather than paying a fixed price. Why? Probably because they assume that the fixed price is not the best price and, when every penny counts, they are willing to work for a better deal.

Polarized buying habits seem to fly in the face of a polarized ability to pay, but the facts seem to speak for themselves.

Still it is shocking to think that the old saw about the rich getting richer seems to be founded in truth. In the U.S.A. the wealthiest 5 percent control 20 percent of the income and that's not all coming from superstar sports figures! In 1970, the top 1 percent controlled only 15 percent of the wealth— only 15 percent! The top 2.3 million Americans have more wealth than the bottom 100 million!

The fastest growing segment is the six million single

moms who are getting by on a median wage of $20,750. How many kids can you feed on that?

When corporate America decided that it was easier to eliminate jobs than to create them, the first to go were, no surprise, the hourly wage earners. But in the past few years the trend has moved up the corporate ladder. In 1994, 62 percent of the downsized jobs belonged to mid-level management!

In case you haven't noticed, this isn't 1950. June Cleaver isn't in your kitchen. She's working, along with millions of other women who are riding in the diamond lanes. Today more than half of all married couples are dual income households.

There is unease in the marketplace as we try to figure out why mass marketing doesn't work, why the tried and true has turned black and blue. It's because the world has changed. The rich got richer and changed their habits while they were doing it. The poor got poorer and smarter. Hard to imagine, but it seems to be so. Likewise, retailers and service providers will have to go with the flow when the toughest thing of all is figuring out just what the heck is the flow and where it's flowing!

MEET ME ON . . .

If I say, "Meet me on ____" do you fill in the blank with "Internet?" If you don't today, do you think you may be thinking that way tomorrow?

Here's a guess.

I predict that the Internet and other forms of electronic communications, including teleconferencing, will result in more in-person meetings, not less. At least I hope so since most of my income depends on folks wanting to share ideas in person. (Only one in seven Americans darkened the door of a bookstore last year! Pretty scary if you are an author!)

I predict that as we meet people and their ideas on the Internet we'll be hungry to meet and greet them in person. I see electronic communication as a stimulant for meetings, rather than a wet blanket. I also predict that meetings will have to offer more opportunities to participate, rather than sitting in rows captive to a "talking head" that from the back of the room seems no more lifelike than if it were on video. (Many large meetings today use video projection to enable the audience sitting in the hinterland to see what would otherwise be a dot of a face on the podium several hundred feet away. Live meetings will have to get better at offering a place where you can meet and share one-on-one with the speaker and his or her ideas.)

RAISING THE BAR

Quality of product is no longer much of an issue. Computer technology and the widespread availability of manufacturing equipment have taken away quality as a competitive point of difference. Made in Japan, Taiwan, or South Korea no longer means junk. The same process that is used to create a quality product anywhere has now been dismantled and shipped to nearly everywhere. Quality is only the ticket to get into the game. It is no longer much of a point of difference.

What is left is service. Our challenge is to deliver quality, engaging service at a price that is competitive.

By our survey two things are true. First, the quality of service has never been higher. And, here's the bad news—the customer has never expected more. The major issue for business in the nineties and on into the next century will be solving the problem of delivering better service at a lower price.

The second half of the service problem will be how to sell the service. Service is often difficult to see or touch. Service has to be sold. If the customer is not aware of the service, or if the customer does not value the service, then we have a problem because service costs money.

POS Point: Service that only adds to the price but not to the customer's satisfaction is almost as bad as giving poor service.

DUH!

One last trend may be the one that kills us—the difficulty of finding and training honest, dependable, reasonably skillful servers to deliver the product.

Recently, educators were asked to list the factors they considered most destructive to education. Among the top issues: decline of family, inability of citizens and educators to recognize the changing role of schools, citizen inattention to social issues.

Mostly as citizens we just complain about public education. The facts actually are cause for optimism. First of all, there is a popular myth that test scores have dropped precipitously. In fact, overall scores have dropped but most, if not all, of the decline can be attributed to large numbers of students who would not have tested at all 20 years ago that are now being encouraged to test. These lower performing groups pull the average down while at the same time selected populations are testing at higher than ever levels.

Our performance compared with other countries remains strong. Studies that show us ranking in twelfth place and lower fail to account for the fact that in other countries only the best students participate in the testing. Plus, the differences in scores are so small as to be statistically insignificant.

Recently, I spoke to the teachers of our local school district. (I am on the school board. They think I'm retired or something!) I talked about economic freedom and the ability for our students to choose how they might live their lives.

I gave the following conversation with a young waitress as an example of our teacher's need to be vigilant role models.

I asked about the lunch specials. She said, "We don't got none."

"Oh! You don't have any," I replied, hoping she would get the message. She did, sort of.

"Well, we don't have no more . . ."

When I paid the check, the change portion was eighty-seven cents. I offered her a twenty and two pennies. Total meltdown. There was no way she was going to be able to figure the change.

Sometimes I feel like everyone's dad. "Miss, you are really a nice person, and I enjoyed having you serve us. If you don't mind my saying, it's really important that you get this change thing figured out. You have a whole life ahead of you, and you would feel so much more powerful if you could count change and talk with people confidently."

She smiled. This could have gone either way. It was clear that she understood and appreciated my intentions.

"I went to school in New Orleans."

Now I don't know how that statement should be interpreted. I will tell you that as long as we allow young people to graduate without insisting that they have complete command of the language of commerce we are denying them the most basic economic freedom.

And that is pretty much the message that I shared with our teachers.

The decline in positive family influence is not insignificant, statistically or otherwise.

Today business operators who are serious about delivering Positively Outrageous Service must, in many instances, serve as both employer and parent, teaching values along with job skills.

If you are looking for answers, there is no point in reading further. The answers are in the mirror, and it's perfectly fine to start at home. When was the last time you made time to listen to what your kid is listening to, to play where your kid is playing, and to visit with your kiddo's friends? If you haven't got a pretty good set of answers, you are the problem.

BOOM

What's that sound in the marketplace? Boomers, they say. Seventy-six million strong and getting older by the moment. On January 1, 1997, a boomer turned 50 every seven-and-a-half seconds. Man, that's a lot of old people! Of course, I'm in the front of the pack, so who am I to cast stones?

It won't be long before boomers, by virtue of declining earning power and eventually declining numbers, will have less and less impact on the economy. For the moment, boomers are it. At least enough so that retailers and service providers will have to pay attention and, maybe, respect! Aging boomers cannot help but have an impact on do-it-yourself industries, vacation providers, and purveyors who support a renewed interest in home activities. Boomers will soon peak in their corporate careers and take that inevitable turn toward home and family.

Yesterday, I met my son for lunch. As we left the restaurant, I thanked him for taking time to join me. "No, Dad. Thank you! It took you even more time. You had to drive into town and wait for me. Thank you!"

In typical boomer fashion, I played dad for just a moment and said, "Son, as I get older I am starting to look at time a little differently. I think of every day as an opportunity that won't repeat. If I missed having lunch with you today, I can't go back and repeat it. If there were ever a day that I didn't tell your mom how much I loved her, how could I ever say, 'I loved you yesterday?' "

Boomers are coming of new age. If you are in business, get ready.

CUSTOMER TIME

Along with the trend toward flattened hierarchies at work comes the corollary of the contingent worker. The numbers change too rapidly to report. Register that as more and more workers are out-placed, more and more workers will serve as contingent employees called to serve the temporary needs of ever skinnier businesses. These contingent workers will be joined by contract workers who will "office" from their homes.

Increasingly we will see independent contractors making use of technology to telecommute, bringing their knowledge to work via copper and fiber lines. Along with this virtual worker, whether full time or contingent, comes a virtual consumer. It's a natural. If you can work via modem, why not shop via modem?

When at last these stay-at-home workers reach a significant number, the impact on business hours will be huge. In the fifties, shopkeepers and bankers could keep short and very regimented hours. For a local store to stay open even an hour longer than was the locally, socially accepted norm was heresy, a cheap competitive shot. As more women moved into the workforce, shopkeepers were forced to extend their hours. Of course, that was only after K-mart employees had eaten their lunch with extended weekday hours and weekend shopping.

Today, retailers and service providers have to be available around the clock or the business will go to the competition. The virtual business will serve the virtual worker, and the virtual worker will become the virtual customer.

I think the virtual customer will be yet another expression of polarized buying habits. When we are in a hurry, or too tired, we'll shop, maybe even play, via modem. When we do venture out, it will be in search of that "experience" that we've been talking about.

This brings us to perhaps the biggest trend of all.

FACE TIME

The impact of personal contact is amplified as technology and downsizing eliminate opportunities for one-on-one service.

As organizations continue to flatten and technology is used to eliminate human involvement, the remaining opportunities for personal contact take on an ever greater importance. Melanie made one of her rare special requests for her birthday; she even suggested where it might be found (in one of those general merchandise catalog stores). While she was picking up office supplies, I slipped a few doors down to see what I could find.

It must have been 60,000 square feet of every imaginable household item. From vacuum to vanity, cooking pots to patio furniture, it was all there. Everything, that is, except human beings. Not a soul in sight. Not a customer, not a clerk, not a nada. My first instinct was to leave—I had walked into a closed store.

Then I saw a huge hanging sign that said, "Order Here." Perfect! A cash register and salesperson. Nope. Just another series of signs that invited me to place my own order.

Step one: Find the item in the catalog.

Step two: Enter the item in the computer. The computer informed me that the item was in stock and politely asked if I wished to order. Press "Y" and "Enter." I did.

The next few steps guided me through the process of swiping my credit card, entering demographic information, and finally, directing me to the pickup area.

In the pickup area, I spied my first human since entering the store. It had purple hair. It had a nose ring. It spent a lot of time looking at its shoes.

If this person had been the fourth or fifth employee that I had talked with, or even noticed, the purple hair and nose ring might not have been all that noticeable. But when you use technology to create operational efficiencies (translate that to "cut staff") you had better darned well be certain that the staff that remains make customers say WOW, not ugh! Technology is amplifying the impact of personal contact.

CRUNCH TIME

Any look at the trends has to include mention of the ever-increasing importance of time. In earlier books, I wrote about the trend to spend time more wisely. If there is a universal mantra that shapes the way consumers make buying decisions, it has to be, "Is it worth it?" This is the ultimate value-checking phrase. It applies to money, of course, but more than ever, consumers are thinking about time and convenience when they make purchase decisions. Time is money. A simple truth in the fifties, a battle cry in the nineties.

The forty-hour work week is dead. Working men average fifty hours per week, working women, forty-two. Assembly-line autoworkers are often taking home $100,000 per year due to incredible amounts of overtime worked. Sixty-two percent of Americans report that they are always, or frequently, rushed at work, and 28 percent of us have not taken a vacation in the past twelve months!

Even supermarket visits have declined by 28 percent since 1989. Do you think busy people don't eat? No, they just make their trips to the supermarket count for more. That and they are eating out more often.

It's interesting to note that one in ten restaurant meals is eaten in a car, and just as interesting to know that in the restaurant industry, it's not the fast feeders who are hurting. Surprise! It's not the high-end, offer-them-an-experience folks either. The pain is being felt in the middle. Get it? Consumers want it fast, or, if they are going to spend their valuable time, they want an experience that makes the sacrifice "worth it."

Quick question: What are you doing to make buying your product an experience? What are you doing to make it "worth it?"

Experience is the word of the day. Smart marketers are focusing on the experience. In 1994, the most widely recognized commercials were the storytelling saga of Tony and Sharon. You remember, Taster's Choice.

In fact, the commercials that ring the bell today are those that tell stories, and those that invite the customer to participate, at least vicariously. Commercials that talk about price, product, packaging, and place will always be a part of the media landscape; but, commercials that tell a story, or make us laugh, are more in keeping with these times when customers will only trade their attention for an experience.

THE POWER OF THE BRAND

If there already isn't enough confusion in the marketplace, let me add one more thought. Service may become branded. Why not? There are a jillion brands that imply a level of service. Why not brand service itself?

The very idea of branding will come under intense scrutiny in the next few years. After all, in-house, generic brands fare quite well when marketed against the national brands. Customers have figured that the power of brands is not the same across all categories. A brand of paper towels may not have the same power to command a higher price as a brand of sandwich or shirt.

Brand will remain important tomorrow for the very rea son they are of value today. Brands help consumers make choices based on predictability of performance. You know how a brand will perform. A well-known brand is a statement of trust. An unknown brand is no brand at all.

WHIPS AND CHAINS

There is an interesting face in the marketplace: category killers. We're talking about the introduction of operations that absolutely dominate the category in terms of price and selection. Toys 'R' Us, CarMax, Home Depot, and Office Max are a few of the familiar leaders. While their appearance may represent a trend, it may be that this is a wave that has already crested. In its place we may look to the virtual category killers, companies that exist only as a catalog, or maybe as a page on the web.

My favorite is Land's End, a relationship without a storefront. The most avant garde has to be Amazon.com, a store that isn't. A store that is always open, pretty friendly, definitely fast, and without a doubt a killer in the category of books. You may have purchased this book from them. If you did, it didn't matter what time of day you shopped, how you dressed, how you paid as long as it wasn't cash or even if my book was present in their warehouse.

That's a new form of dominance. Something for ma and pa on Main Street to think about.

DR. DEMING . . . DANGEROUS?

The BS seminar of the eighties was "Stress Management." Now who in their right mind would want to "manage" stress? No one!

Still, organizations paid out a collective gazillion bucks for the privilege of having a platform professional relieve them of more training dollars than stress. But the topic was hot, and you have to spend those training bucks somewhere, so why not on "Stress Management?"

"Stress Relief," or "Handling Stress," any title other than "Stress Management" would have at least been more intellectually straightforward. Excess stress is more a sign of plain old bad management than the result of an alien plot to drive managers bonkers. A good course on management fundamentals would have served the world a heck of a lot better.

I hope most of the meetings were held poolside. That's the best way I know to "manage" stress!

Now we have an even bigger and, if possible, trendier topic grabbing up the bucks and racking up training hours.

"Ladies and gentlemen, I give you the newest, hottest,

trendiest, and probably least likely-to-have-any-impact-on-organizations program of the nineties (drumroll, please) T.Q. followed by anything!"

Tweaked your nose, didn't I? Well, someone had to intervene and make you look before you went completely off the deep Deming end.

I don't mean to attack either the good doctor or his wonderful teachings. But I certainly do intend to attack the results of the man's ideas being interpreted by a legion of consultants who seem to be pouring out of the woodwork.

Here's a fine example.

In what has become one of the biggest business books of the year, and I refer mainly to size not sales, Deming is quoted, probably out of context, as saying, "We must do whatever it takes to stamp out variation."

Baloney!

We shouldn't be stamping out variation. We should be encouraging it!

In a manufacturing environment, variation can indeed be a tremendous liability. It would be closer to the truth in this age of computer-controlled manufacturing to finger "uncontrolled" variation as a liability. Controlled variation is, or can be, a competitive edge.

In Henry Ford's day, it was the elimination of variance that brought efficiency to the process, lowering price, increasing affordability, and eventually creating even more sales.

In those days an any-color-you-want-as-long-as-it's-black mentality made perfectly good sense.

But today, using computers to control variation, manufacturers are capable of short-run mass production that allows every piece to be customized. Now there's a form of variation that is a tremendous benefit to both producer and consumer alike.

The real fraud of Deming's deputies is that too often they

forget that we are not living in a manufacturing economy. Ours is a service economy.

Service does not benefit from eliminating variance. In fact, eliminating variance can have just the opposite effect. Think for a moment about the things that bother you most about customer service. Most of your peeves come from a misguided attempt to stamp out variance.

"Sorry, we can't do that."

"It's our policy not to allow substitutions."

"I don't know." (This is an example of limiting employees' ability to respond in an attempt to eliminate the possibility that they might, for goodness sake, make a decision!)

And don't forget the all-time favorite, "It's not my job."

Add in the millions of monotonous greetings that corporate thinkers force on servers and you have a veritable crisis of too little variance!

"We actually heard this gem. "It's a great day at _____. My name is _____ and it will be a true pleasure to serve you." Isn't that a barf-in-your-shoes abomination?

The point is simple. Jump on the wrong bandwagon and, even though you'll have plenty of company, you're still going in the wrong direction. Quality customer service depends not on eliminating variance but on handling it better than the other guy. Have it your way!

WHAT'S THIS POS?

Positively Outrageous Service is all about wrapping an experience around a service transaction. Done right, Positively Outrageous Service is the service story that you can't wait to tell. It is a WOW on a random basis.

You don't even attempt to dish up a serving of POS for every customer every time. You couldn't do it. It wouldn't be prudent. Besides, remove the element of surprise and you don't have POS. Remove the surprise and you've got raised expectations, consistently great service maybe, but not Positively Outrageous Service.

In the coming chapters we'll find out how to deliver on a promise like POS. But first, let's find out if you are ready.

IS THIS POS?

A former client of ours had as a slogan: "Good enough seldom is." They neither believed nor practiced this slogan, but it certainly turned me around. I remember the first time I walked into our little restaurant after hearing this "good enough seldom is" stuff.

I had always been one to pick up trash on the way into the store. My dad taught me that. Maybe I had missed a bit of the message because often I would pick up the really big pieces and ignore the little stuff. Or maybe I would get the trash close to the door and look at the stuff over along the fence line, at the trash that could be considered the neighbor's trash, and say, "Well, that's good enough."

Well, good enough seldom is and now, with that silly slogan ringing in my ears, I could no longer settle for the big pieces. I had to get the little stuff, too!

It got to the point where I think our crew would see me coming and toss trash out the door to slow me down and give them a little extra time to get the place in shape!

This whole thing makes me think about Positively Outrageous Service, and this I believe to be true. If you are the type to walk by trash in the parking lot or just pick up the big stuff and say, "This is good enough for now," I don't think there is a snowball's chance in hell that POS is going to come to your place.

I think of all the bosses who would walk past trash, leave a restroom dirty, or a copy machine jammed, doing nothing more than making a mental note that they need to send someone to handle it. I think about those folks and imagine them wondering why the staff doesn't seem to be getting the concept of Positively Outrageous Service. And I realize that POS isn't going to happen everywhere.

That is good news and bad news. The bad news is that POS isn't for everyone. The good news is that if you are the kind of boss who has a basic respect for those who serve and a deep commitment to running a quality shop, then POS is for you. For you, POS will be a competitive advantage that will blow you right by the service wanna-bes!

SEVEN

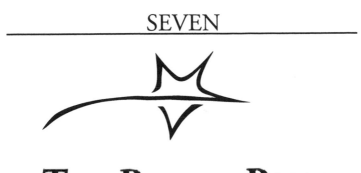

THE PEOPLE PART

"Treat your competition kindly;
hire poorly."

I n my third book, *Positively Outrageous Service and Showmanship,* I said that the job of management is to hire—not just until the schedule is full, but until it is full with winners. Then, keep hiring! Follow Scott's Law of Expansion:

A business will expand in direct proportion to the number of winning employees that can be found.
Hire all the winners, get all the business!

The key to hiring is not just to hire; you must audition. Good managers audition because it tells the employee that getting this job won't be easy and keeping it will be a badge of honor.

The following is an excerpt from *Positively Outrageous Service and Showmanship.* It is included here because, as Thoreau said, "That which is once done well is done forever." This is a valuable insight to hiring. For those who want a more in-depth look, buy the book!

~∾~

HOW TO CONDUCT AN AUDITION

Use a few tricks and a few more techniques to turn an ordinary interview into an extraordinary audition.

Schedule auditions. Because they are so important, they should never be held on the spur of the moment. And auditions, or try-outs, heighten the effect.

The best at hiring winners tend to make a big deal out of auditions. By extending an invitation to audition, or to try out, they let the applicant know right up front that the hiring decision is so very important that it is an honor to even be invited to try.

. . . Auditions create a sense of competition. Whenever possible, applicants who are invited to audition should be made aware of the competition. They should see exactly who they are trying to beat out for the job. They could even be invited to audition simultaneously to further heighten the sense of competition as well as to drive home the point that the job is desirable, a factor that will ultimately impact turnover.

Best of all, simultaneous auditions let you see instantly who will fold in the heat of battle. This is very important for jobs that require high customer contact.

. . . Have top management involved in the audition process. This makes the point that auditions are important—to current employees as well as the applicants. In fact, in addition to management and the applicants, current employees should also be a part of the audition process. It's good for them to see again that they are special to have made the cut. That, and a close look at the competition, goes a long way toward putting the value of their jobs into sharp perspective.

We let our employees vote on new hires. It certainly makes the point to applicants that they are not just taking a job, they are joining a team and the team has a vital interest in both their performance and their success.

. . . Auditions are more than an interview; they are a performance.

(At this point, we introduce five exercises—monologue, phone call, echo, mirror, and simultaneous story—to use in the audition. The point to these exercises is to assess the applicant's ability to "fit" your organization. We'll continue with selected excerpts related to monologue, to give you a better understanding of its relevance to POS.)

. . . Nearly every business requires employees to recite some type of monologue. It can be a simple greeting, a standardized sales pitch or a canned telemarketing script. Most of the time it is just plain boring.

. . . While new employees may need a standard patter to help make certain that they cover all the bases, the rest of us need to be protected not from beginners but from those folks who never get it right.

Ask applicants to deliver a monologue that is your standard service patter or some variation on the theme. It could be as simple as "Hi! Welcome to Acme. My name is _____, and I'll be available to help you find anything you need and to answer questions about our products. What project are you working on today?"

Invite the applicant to deliver the lines straight or personalize them to suit. Better yet, do the entire routine with the applicant interacting with several types of customers. Your part: Observe how well the applicant senses the needs of the different "customers" and adapts the spiel to fit the situation.

As a side idea, it will also be helpful to throw in any related skills that may influence the hiring decision. If the job requires basic math or counting skills, then make them a part of the process.

. . . The best addition to the monologue is the requirement to handle an angry or complaining customer. Role practice the situation and quickly discover the applicant's natural abilities for conflict resolution. Does he buckle under pressure? Does she attack, rather than hold steadfast to "the customer is always right" mentality?

. . . Just be careful not to use the term "role play." To many, it communicates that the situation is much less serious than it is. Role "practice" indicates that, while humor may be appropriate, the exercise is not designed to screen for comedic ability.

Also be careful that whatever you require as part of the audition is truly a required behavior on the job. See your local human resources professional if you would rather hear a thousand reasons why you cannot do anything out of the ordinary and why you are required by law to continue hiring people who haven't a prayer of being successful working for you.

~~~

POS Point: Even when the applicant has left you breathless with his/her skills and experience, no hire should be more than an extended trial period. The job offer should be provisional based on continued impressive performance.

Today POS is practiced worldwide by client-believers in industries from travel to technology, retailing to auto rental. Unfortunately, talking about POS turns out to be a whole lot easier than getting ordinary people to actually deliver on the promise.

So why don't your employees reach out to establish warmer relations with your customers? I can think of at least five reasons: Personality mismatch, lack of skills, misunderstood objectives, lack of time and tools, and conflicting reinforcement.

PERSONALITY

Ron Zemke identified a personality trait that he calls "customer contact tolerance." This, says Zemke, is the psychological ability to tolerate one customer after another without going absolutely nuts. Indifferent service may not really be a matter of not liking people; it could be a case of not being able to tolerate so much of the direct, relentless contact so common to the industry.

POS Point: If you have employees who can't tolerate high customer contact, no amount of training or reinforcement is going to turn on their charm.

During breakfast at Disney's Contemporary Resort, my red pen died. It was a slow and agonizing death with red ink leaking all over my hand. After breakfast I headed to the gift shop to find a replacement with no such luck. Actually, I got plenty lucky. Not at buying a pen, but in meeting a wonderful lady named Odila. (Gosh! I hope I have the spelling right!)

"Sorry, sir. We don't sell red pens. But maybe I have one."

In the middle of a busy shift, this wonderful woman took time to rummage through the drawer beneath the cash register. She called a co-worker at another shop in the hotel. Then another and another and another until finally, she said, "I think I have the problem solved!"

Within a matter of seconds, I was presented with a red pen. It did not come with a cap. (No big deal. And, gee whiz! Can beggars really be choosers?)

No problem. She whipped the cap from her own pen and sent me on my way with a pen, a cap, and a smile. No charge!

Believe it or not, this level of service is routine for the Contemporary Resort. I don't know how or where they manage to find so many customer lovers, but whoever does the hiring to find them and keep them deserves a medal!

In the search for employees who have high customer tolerance, many of our clients have given up interviewing in favor of auditioning. Auditioning prospective employees gives employers a chance to evaluate job candidates as they handle real or simulated customer service situations.

SERVICE IS AN ART

It's also a matter of skill. Lack of customer service skills is another reason why employees often miss opportunities to make customers say, "WOW!" Think about it. We are asking employees to establish a personal relationship with a total stranger.

Normal human beings avoid doing things that make them uncomfortable or that could cause them embarrassment. Your employees need a few good opening lines to help them get the ball rolling. We taught our employees several funny or friendly things to say to those customers who looked like they would like to play or who needed a little cheer. One easy-to-try technique we call "inflation." In our restaurant we'd inflate the amount, the amount tendered, and the change.

"That's $210 out of $500, and it looks like $290 is your change. Don't spend it all in one place!" Of course, we'd be handling all of a five-dollar bill.

We adopted funny names for our products calling eggs cackleberries and milk moo juice. Of course, not everyone wants to play; but, when they do, it's important that you have provided your team with a few good lines so they will be ready to take advantage of opportunities to play.

Since we are talking about creativity here, we're going to "tell on" Sally, our resident bean-counter. Sally was a den mother when her youngest was of scouting age. The good news? The kids absolutely adored her. The bad news? They loved her so much they wouldn't leave her alone.

Finally, unable to stand it, she bought a neck brace, wore it to the monthly meeting, and told the scoutmaster that due to health problems, she would have to resign!

YOUR MISSION, SHOULD YOU DECIDE TO . . .

Lack of clear objectives is another major cause of indifferent customer service. Let's amend this to also read, "poor example." This is absolutely true. If management doesn't put customers first, ahead of phone calls and schedules, why would anyone think that employees would behave differently?

When management go into the stores, do they serve customers? Do they play with customers? Do they do things that could be interpreted as service for the team? If the answer is "no," stop looking at your team for customer service and take a long look into the mirror.

One of my favorite clients is John King of J. Kings Food Service Professionals in Oakdale, New York. Every employee, all ninety-five of them from warehouse to executive suite, has a business card. John says that an employee who is not important enough to have a business card is not important enough to handle his customers.

Here's a touch of POS from John himself: Each year he takes a few of his customers on a fact-finding mission in search of ideas for improving their businesses. John's theory is that if he can help his customers improve their sales, the inevitable result is that they will buy more from J. Kings.

Smart man that John King. Maybe that's why he was named Innovator of the Year by his industry association.

WORK SHOULD BE . . .

If you completed the above sentence by saying "work" instead of "fun," you've discovered yet another stumbling block to Positively Outrageous Service. Lack of time and tools kills any chance that either the server or the served will get much out of the transaction. Face it. When stores are understaffed (you could interpret that as employees overworked), there is no point in expecting Positively Outrageous Service.

Employees who can barely keep up with the crush aren't going to take time to be playful or go the extra mile.

POS Point: Take a serious look at your operation and ask yourself, "Am I choking great customer service by scheduling too lean?"

My dad always said, "You control your volume with a pencil." What he meant was that if you only schedule enough staff to handle low volume, there is no way that volume will grow. The same is true for service, and today, service is the competitive difference. Think about it. Are your prices really much lower than those down the street? Are your products really any different? If not, what is the difference? Service! And service, beyond the merely passable, won't happen when the crew must run just to stay in place.

BUT YOU SAID . . .

Perhaps one of the biggest reasons for poor or indifferent service is conflicting reinforcement. In the end, people do the things that are rewarded. Period. You may wonder why people do stupid things. Simple. We often reward stupid. Reward stupid, get stupid.

"But I never reward indifferent service!"

Maybe. But do you measure and reward really great service? If treating customers indifferently gets the same reaction from the boss as loving them to death, many folks think, "Why not just take the easy way out? Why make an effort when the effort goes unrewarded?"

POS Point: Failing to reinforce great service is de facto reinforcement of poor service.

A woman driving on IH-10 in San Antonio was startled when her rear window disintegrated while driving. The terrified woman pulled off the freeway into the parking lot of Carrabba's Italian Grill. She went in to call the police, saying her window had been shot out.

While comforting her for nearly an hour, the employees not only cleaned up the glass, but installed a temporary plastic cover since it was raining at the time.

She wrote the local paper, saying, "I hope you can give these wonderful people the recognition they deserve."

And the managing partner, Chuck Criswell, replied, "We want to be part of the community. We want to make San Antonio a little better."

The most difficult and important responsibilities of management are to communicate expectations, provide the training and tools needed to get the job done, and manage performance through positive reinforcement.

The sum total of an organization's policies and procedures along with the way things "really get done" constitutes what some companies call their corporate culture. Fair enough, but this culture is a system for managing performance. The performance management system is the sum total of influences on employee performance (i.e., pay plans, the physical work environment, contests, reports—everything that serves to provide consequences for behavior, both positive and negative).

Whether or not you make the customer connection is not a simple matter. It is a series of simple matters that together determine team performance. Making the customer connection is more than creating policy or producing motivating videos. The hard work of management, the work that really counts, is creating systems where making the customer connection is more than a slogan—it's the sole focus of a well-thought system of good performance management that follows great hiring.

FACE TIME

There is a tremendously valuable asset going to waste in your organization—face time.

Face time is that old real estate principle of highest and best use applied to the boss. Even in this egalitarian world where the boss is known by Pam or Chuck, customers (internal and external) still put a premium on time spent with the boss. Face time is nothing less, but a whole lot more, than the mere presence of El Jefe, The Chief Honcho, The Boss, The Grand Poobah.

Face time is important for three reasons—status, example, and intelligence. More about these in a moment.

Office time rarely has the same value as face time. Offices are too often a place to hide. If the boss really has superior expertise, then why isn't that expertise in the field or on the floor where it can be shared? If the boss is only marginal, then maybe the office is the place where he or she is least likely to do damage. Otherwise, most of what gets done in offices either could be done by someone who has a much lower face value or, as is often the case, work that really needn't be done at all.

Pagers are a variation on the theme. Pagers are too often an excuse to be someplace you shouldn't be. Period.

The Employment of Face

Face time puts the boss in direct contact with the customer. Even at the lowest level, the boss's face has incredible value. When we owned our little restaurant (where four dollars would get you lunch and change), people wanted to be recognized by the owner. They wanted to know that when they walked in the door, the owner, not a clerk, cook, or assistant, would call them by name.

A restaurant that serves mediocre food, but where the boss is omnipresent, will beat out a fine dining establishment where the boss never makes an appearance. Think about the businesses that make you feel good and I guarantee that the boss is likely to be present much of the time. Better yet, I gurantee that the boss is right out front, maybe even knows you by name. Right? Right!

You visit the White House. What do your neighbors want to know? See what I mean?

You travel to Hollywood. What do your friends ask about? The weather? No way!

The same goes for your business. Your customers want to see Y-O-U! You don't have to be a celebrity to have face value. Like the Wizard of Oz might say, "What you need is a title." "Boss" will do nicely.

When we visit Boccone's Restaurant, we know three things: The food and service will be out of this world; we'll have to wait for a parking space and then wait for a table; and we'll see Al or Mary Helen, probably both. And it's the latter fact that accounts for the first two on the list.

Face time also has immeasurable value in terms of the training that inevitably occurs. Look, all learning is by doing. The things your people are most likely to do (learn) are the things that they see in the work environment and try for themselves. This means that all the other people at work are, in fact, your training program. It also follows that since the boss is, well, the boss, he carries a pretty hefty face value, making the boss the most potent training aid of all.

Be careful! This sword cuts both ways. The last thing a boss can get away with is a "do as I say, not what I do," attitude. Like it or not, what the boss does, the troops do. Grouchy boss, grouchy troops. Boss quality-minded, troops watch quality. Boss cleans break room, troops clean break room! (This stuff is powerful, but not perfect!)

The important thing to remember is that floor time isn't necessarily face time. If you are working the floor out of sight and earshot of the employees, your time, at least as far as the employees are concerned, has no more value than that of another body on the clock. You may still have face time with the customer, but it only counts if the customer knows that you are the boss.

Late one night I slipped into the office in underwear and tennis shoes. (I know that's an odd combination, but the office is attached to the house and the dog doesn't seem to mind.) The phone rang and I answered, "T. Scott Gross and Company," just like the staff had taught me!

"Can I order a book at this number?"

"Yes, ma'am. You certainly can!"

"I need it by tomorrow. I've looked at our local bookstore, and they are out."

"Well, if you live in the San Antonio area, I'm going to the airport and could drop it off to you."

"I live in Kansas City."

"Sorry, not that airport! Tell me, why do you need the book tomorrow?"

"I read an article about Positively Outrageous Service and got so excited about it that I called a staff meeting for the morning. I just assumed I could buy the book locally."

"Well, I bet I can help you with a few of the concepts."

We talked for nearly half an hour as she took notes, asked questions, and generally became a semiexpert on POS.

"You've been so helpful!" she said. "I can't believe that someone working the order desk this late at night would be so knowledgeable! Tell your boss that you deserve a raise!"

I was so proud of myself for being a good order-taker I didn't tell her that I had also written the book!

Face time. No value.

The third value of face time is intelligence gathering. All of the mystery shoppers, 800 lines, comment cards, and focus groups in the world won't tell you half as much as will your loyal customers. Nothing beats asking customers face-to-face what they like about your product or service or how they would change it if they were in charge. Customers will spill their guts helping you beat your competition if they think they are dealing with someone who can and will make a change for the better.

There is such a thing as telephone face time, too! A few minutes on the phone every day, calling customers to ask "How are we doing?", has more value than an entire day spent poring over numbers from last period. Last period is history. A real customer on the line is opportunity!

Face time is leadership in action. Tom Peters called it MBWA—Management By Walking Around. I call it MBWA—Management By Working Around. Nothing beats firsthand experience and MBWA is definitely it.

Smart managers will make a point of scheduling themselves to work a shift or two with the troops.

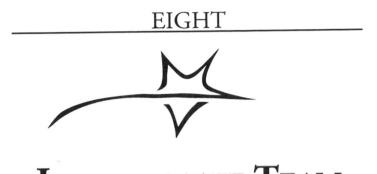

EIGHT

LEADING THE TEAM

Have you ever been to Germany? How about Fredericksburg, Texas? We had just come from a short ride to Fredericksburg, about as German a town as you can find this side of the Atlantic. In the center of town stands a giant maypole. Maypoles are similar to totem poles. They give the history of the town and its people through a series of two-dimensional symbols and pictures. In Fredericksburg, as in most German towns, the maypole includes references to the kind of work done by the local people. After all, work accounts for the biggest portion of our lives.

The history of work is about to come full circle. In days past, people didn't work strictly defined hours or report to limited locations. The idea of working in a factory, doing the same thing, often a single repetitive motion, is an aberration in the history of man.

Now, work has evolved to a matter of shifting tasks completed in multiple locations. A century ago, we would be talking about farming and ranching. Today the definition applies to many occupations. The idea of a factory was too radical to comprehend decades ago when the vast majority worked the fields, following schedules and task lists dictated more by season and sunlight than by time clock and assembly line.

POS Point: Humans are naturally inclined to work independently.

The Wall Street Journal reports that "Some Busy Employees Are Getting Busier with Parallel Careers." (Time out. I rest my case.) The article, dated Aug. 13, 1996, talks about people who are taking on dual careers, and not just for the money. What the article refers to as "casserole careers" speaks to our ability to handle a multitude of unrelated tasks. Humans are quite capable of extraordinary activity. We are not genetically designed to "veg" on the couch. More important, we are not designed to "veg" at work.

Work that is not challenging kills. Compare any tough, fast-paced job with one that is mind-numbingly boring. You know which of the two is most likely to wear you down. Humans need challenge. We are by nature problem solvers, so much so that when faced with an abundance of problems, we say, "No problem!" and create more problems!

When my business is perfect, I look for a new product or adventure to make things complicated. You do the same. People thrive when challenged and wilt when left to do the same old thing over and over again.

AN UNNATURAL ACT!

Most of work today is organized around a product or service that is designed to look the same as the one that came before. Deming was right when he invented the idea of statistical process control to dramatically raise the level of quality. Too bad the theory doesn't hold up when we are dealing with customer service where instead of stamping out variance, the smart operators are encouraging it!

Work that is built around a bureaucracy fosters a liability of scale (not economy of scale)! An example is organization charts that encourage hiring because they represent power to the bosses who are high enough in the organization to have their name typed in one of the boxes. The more little boxes under your name, the more digits on the paycheck. Simple as that!

Worse is the fact that, by its very nature, a job discourages accountability as most are arranged around a task or function rather than a result. How many times have you seen a great idea spoiled by the need to run it past an army of bureaucrats, each covering their anatomy and doing their job? Some will even tell you that it is their job to question, to act as a brake on risk.

From the top comes an even more perverted view of work. Witness the late fad of downsizing. A CEO who must downsize is making a huge admission that things were out of line before the ax began to fall. If the bodies that were tossed overboard were unnecessary, why were they on the payroll in the first place? If they are necessary, just exactly how and where is quality likely to suffer? Has Peter been robbed to pay Paul? When will the note become due?

Downsize is the right size? Not even!

In a study done for hospitals by Deloitte & Touche, 81 percent of hospitals participating reported that employee morale was a major problem. The second-highest ranking problem was concern over downsizing. Looks to me to be one and the same!

Cutting jobs without rethinking the way work gets done, or what work gets done at all, leaves gigantic holes in the organization that causes quality to suffer and people to burn slowly to the ground.

Look at the numbers. Very interesting. In 1995 there were 11.17 managers per 100 employees. In 1990 that ratio was nearly identical at 11.83. What does that tell you? It tells me that nothing has changed. Internal jobs have been re-engineered to give the few who remained more decision-making authority to the point that they are now considered management. Plus, since even after re-engineering, or downsizing, the work still needed to be done, the worker bees, who were cut, in many cases became outsource providers. So the managers ended up staying because someone has to supervise the now "contingent" workforce.

The decline in managers was greatest in the service industry where the ratio went from 10.69 per one hundred employees in 1989 to 9.35 per hundred in 1994.

In construction the number of managers per hundred employees only fell 2.18 percent.

So what really got downsized? The organizational chart and little else. And who got hurt? People who were ill-prepared to become self-managed contingent workers.

This is only a temporary glitch in the history of industry as the workforce learns again to work on its own and corporations learn to get the most out of contingent workers.

What else suffers? Probably an organization's long-term ability to compete. Start swinging the ax and folks get nervous. Simultaneously, the team realizes that their loyalty to the corporation is not reciprocated. And look who is first out the door—the longest-term employee, the one who best understands the industry. The one with the most experience, the one with the best network—gone!

And what does innovation require other than a committed, competent workforce that knows how to communicate in and around the proper channels? The history of great innovation is the history of skunk works and internal risk-taking, something that the new worker is least likely to attempt or be successful at doing.

The challenge of the new organization is learning how to manage a mobile, often contingent workforce. How do you build commitment and networking capability among a workforce that may be with you for today's project and with your competitor tomorrow?

The employees who are left must become more effective. That requires freedom and encouragement to make key decisions, information to make good decisions, and a stake in the outcome.

WHEN WORK HAS MEANING

When work means something, it becomes a labor of love. When work has meaning, there is a chance that it will also be fun.

POS Point: When work has meaning, more work gets done.

Riding with my then ten-year-old son, I asked how he had performed on a test at school.

"I did okay. I missed seven questions and got an eighty-six."

"I'm surprised. When you and I went over the material, you answered every question perfectly. You knew them all."

To prove my point, I began asking him questions that I remembered. I was blown away to discover that now, two days later, he could barely answer half of them correctly.

"Son! You could answer all of these just two days ago! What has happened?"

"Dad, I don't need to know this stuff anymore. The test was yesterday!"

Duh! And here I thought that the purpose of school was to learn things that might be useful in your life. Now a ten-year-old was pistol-whipping me with the reality that the purpose of school is to memorize data long enough to spit it out on a test!

Is it possible that your employees are suffering from the same malady? Lack of purpose? For example, I love the story about the three stone carvers.

One was drearily chipping away at a huge block of stone when a passing traveler asked what he was doing.

"Shaping this stone," came the somber reply. "It's killing me one whack at a time."

A little further down the road was another mason. The traveler, upon noting that this carver was working a little faster than the other and seemed noticeably happier, again asked what the man was doing.

"I'm shaping this stone for a building!"

Still further along the road was a third crafts- man who was both swinging his hammer and sing- ing as he carved.

"You seem awfully happy for a man working so hard in this heat," said the traveler. "What are you doing?"

"I'm building a cathedral!"

What are your employees building? Better yet, why are they building?

In a classic study, supervisors were asked to list what mo- tivated workers. Then workers in all lines of endeavor were asked to respond to the same question. Surprisingly, the two lists were nowhere near identical. I would publish the survey results except for two reasons. First, a survey of workers in general would most likely not reflect the feelings of the work- ers in your industry; and, second, because even an accurate survey of your industry would not represent your employees individually.

We found out, simply by asking, that even in our own small company, no two team players come anywhere close to being similarly motivated.

You might think that what turns on workers are the money and benefits. If you thought so, you would be right, but only partly so. In a survey of lottery players, it was discov- ered that eight of ten said that if they won the lottery, they would continue to work. Wanna know why? People like to work. The news gets even better when you learn what it is about work that they like, and money doesn't even make the top ten!

Asked what turns them on about work, people cited things like being in the know, the opportunity to learn new skills, and a chance to work with others as top motivators.

Unfortunately, as the workplace changes at an ever more rapid pace in response to technology and competition, workers are feeling more that their identity comes less from where they work than from the work they do.

Years ago when I had a real job, if you asked me where I would be working when I turned sixty-five, I would have pointed at the blue building on IH-10 in San Antonio and said, "Right there!"

Why? Because I strongly identified with the company. In those days you couldn't much tell the difference between me and the company logo. Today, I am not a "where-I-work" but a "what-I-do." And that is true for a growing percentage of the workforce. A survey reported in *Fortune* magazine said that an astounding 47 percent of the workforce "either dislike or are ambivalent about the company they work for, up from 34 percent" just four years earlier.

What is the biggest motivator of today's worker? Control over their own time. Today, the biggest motivator is freedom. Not the freedom to retire but the freedom to put work in perspective. Workers want to give more meaning to that part of life that exists outside of work.

By putting more value on their lives as individuals, workers are demanding more meaning from the time they spend while at work. People are beginning to seek a work life that is in harmony with the rest of the day.

Employees list flexible scheduling and the ability to bank time off among the most important benefits.

Should all this really matter to the employer?

Some years ago, I waltzed into my boss's office with what I thought was a terrific idea for an incentive program for our hourly workers. I laid out the plan and stood back to catch the praise that wasn't about to come.

"We already have an incentive plan," he said taking me totally by surprise.

"We do?"

"Yep! They do their job, they get to keep it."

That was only one of many times that I left his office with my tail dragging.

Stupid!

One study reported that fully 84 percent of employees surveyed admitted that they were not working to their full ability.

When we ask our audiences of managers how much more work their team players could produce if they were really motivated, the average response is 30 percent. Get it? Our audiences think that their employees are only working at 70 percent capacity. That's an incredible motivation gap, the difference between what gets done and what could be done if only the workforce were motivated to effort closer to their full capability.

IT'S THE WORK, STUPID!

No. It is the stupid work!

Do you know how to kill a sixteen-year-old? Easy. Sneak into the fast-food restaurant of the world and remove the amount tendered key from the cash registers. When they open in the morning, be first in line, and place an order in the amount of, say, $2.28. Hand the clerk a five dollar bill and three pennies. Odds are that he or she will self-destruct!

Working in our little restaurant one day, a sixteen-year-old employee was watching over my shoulder as I quickly dispatched orders on the drive-through.

"How do you do that?" he inquired of my register technique. "Easy. Instead of entering the amount tendered, I just hit the amount tendered key, the drawer opens, and I count back the change. It's much easier."

"No. How do you know how much change to give them?" he puzzled.

"It's a secret! Only odd people know how to do this!"

Do you want to know why kids can't count change and do a few other things that their parents take as a matter of fact? We don't let them count change anymore!

True story. I walked into a Taco Bell and waited patiently in line while the guy in front of me proceeded to order $19.10 worth of tacos and such. When he finished ordering, the young woman behind the register announced the total. He fished through his pockets looking for a dime to hand over with the twenty dollar bill.

For whatever reason, the amount tendered key malfunctioned. The poor clerk was totally baffled.

You can see why. A total of $19.10 and she is offered a twenty and a dime. Okay. Pencils down!

I thought that she was going to cry when along came the assistant manager who gently moved her out of the way saying, "You can't do this one, Evelyn. Let me handle it."

I thought that he was being a bit rude, but was glad to see someone available to take charge. With that, he reached into his shirt pocket and took out a pocket calculator!

Thanks to computerized sales transaction technology, counting change is a lost art. Not many years ago we required new restaurant employees to memorize the price of each and every menu item, including so-called "odd-ball" orders, before we ever let them step behind the counter. Today, we have a register key for every conceivable order. Sometimes the key is marked with a little picture of the item to make using it even easier.

It's no small wonder when clerks and servers are totally baffled when a customer asks for an item or combination that cannot be keyed using the little pictures on the register.

POS Point: When you make jobs so idiot-proof that only idiots can stand to do them,

you have no right to complain about the quality of the help!

I, for one, would not mind seeing us re-engineer the workplace with the intention of adding complications just to make the job at hand challenging enough to keep regular people from going absolutely bonkers. The added benefit would be that when customers made "out-of-the-norm requests," employees would be able to comfortably handle them.

Along with the requirement to think that comes with every properly engineered job comes the requirement for management to empower and take a few small risks. Eliminating variance (make that "risk") through standardizing the job process and focusing employees into narrow, mind-numbing tasks is another way to offend thinking customers.

Here's an aside. Only 12 percent of customers think that they have a great deal of influence over the level of service that they receive. I guess that's because they, too, work at dummied-down jobs and are therefore willing to accept being told such nonsense as, "That's our policy" or "I don't know."

We walked into a well-known department store with the intention of purchasing two new serving bowls to match our stoneware.

I picked up a piece from our pattern that was on display and said to the clerk with a smile, "Hi! Can you find us a couple of bowls to match this pattern?"

"We don't have any. All we have is a matching blue or a plain white. Which would you like?"

"I'd like two that match this pattern."

"We only have blue or plain white." (She's thinking by now that I have a hearing impairment when, in fact, we are dealing with a service impairment.)

"Is this pattern no longer available?"

"Not here."

"But you have the rest of the pieces. How could we go about getting a couple of bowls that match?" (This was actually more dare than threat.)

"Well, they may have them at one of our other stores," she said, thinking that she was close to getting this interruption out of her department and her hair.

"Great idea! How could we find that out?"

Now she was really PO'd, but she had finally figured out that I didn't come in to "not" buy bowls and that getting me out would be a tad more difficult than dialing for security.

"I'll call."

Her frosty response made me thirsty for a Midori margarita, but I decided to settle for the sport of getting what I wanted and perhaps teaching her a small lesson about customer service in the process. (As I write, "Teach Your Children Well" is on the CD, a Crosby, Stills, and Nash leftover. This clerk's parents must have been making out in the Chevy instead of listening!)

She attacked the telephone. "They have one at North Star. Do you want them to hold it for you?"

"What about the other one? We need two." I dug in for the long haul.

"Would you rather have one bowl that matched your set or none?" said Ms. Frosty.

"I didn't drive all this way to buy one bowl. We need two. The pattern is open stock, so I know that if you are resourceful, we can find another." I smiled my warmest toother. "Got any ideas?"

"I'll call another store," replied Ms. Congeniality.

I had ruined an otherwise quiet Saturday.

She attacked the phone again. "They have two at Rolling Oaks!" Now even she was excited. She was smiling, and I was not quite certain why. Maybe because she thought we would leave. Maybe because she had had a win and was actually feeling good over her ability to solve a customer's problem. (Or is that solve a problem customer?)

"Great! You did good!" I lied to the Ice Queen.

"Will you be able to pick them up today? No, I have a better idea."

You could almost see the little light go on. I knew without waiting for her next words that she had experienced a conversion of sorts—from mindless, gum-chewing clerk to customer service champion.

Now she was speaking into the phone with authority, "Listen. Take those bowls up to customer service and have them shipped to . . ."

She gave our address and credit card number and finished by saying into the phone, "I know this is a bit unusual, but you can do it."

How many customers could be so much more satisfied and how many employees would be inclined to stay at their jobs if we made a concerted effort to make working less of an idiot-proof proposition? What could we do for service if we simply refused to lower our expectations and insisted that employees use that magnificent brain that we hire but so seldom put to work?

WHY YOU CAN'T LET GO

The management gurus all say to do it. You know that you should. "But, darn it," you say to yourself, "this is a tough business. Empowerment is nice as a concept when you are dealing with a pristine environment of executives in paneled offices, but this is the real world where the rubber meets the road. There is no room for screwups. Let's get real! You have to have systems and policies and a whole lot of luck just to keep the doors open. How the heck do you empower people who may or may not even show up for work?"

Fair question.

You don't.

The CEO of Harley-Davidson made the point that when

you empower idiots, you get bad decisions faster. He's probably right.

There is a lot that can be done to get your employees to bring their brains to work. But, there are two basic problems.

Problem number one: Letting loose of the reins.

Problem number two: Getting someone else to grab them!

LETTING GO

Split the empowerment issue in half and a big chunk of the problem falls right into the lap of management. Face it. Not everyone in management is willing, or even wants, to turn in his keys to the fire truck. Jingling those keys, wearing the hat, and driving at breakneck speed to the most recent two-alarm are thrilling!

So reason number one for not letting go: We like being the problem-solver who rides to the rescue and saves the day.

Some of us like to think of ourselves as being totally indispensable. We folks haven't taken a real vacation in years. We can't. The world would collapse if we were out of pocket for more than twenty-four hours on a slow day. We wear beepers as badges of courage, little testosterone meters that hang from the belt.

Of course, we are the same folks who die early. We are also the worst managers in the business. How can we possibly claim to be running a business when it is clear that it is the business that is running us?

We are left to face the ugly truth that it is not easy to attract the most gifted and the most qualified, especially if we are working in an industry known for asking people to work long hours in tough environments often at wages that are hardly generous. Does this fairly well describe your business? If so, welcome to the club!

In a gajillion or so speaking engagements, I can hardly recall a client that hasn't implied at least once that their industry was different, more difficult than the average bear. Bologna! (Or baloney!)

What if even 20 percent of your folks could and would make intelligent, customer-first decisions, the kind not covered in the operations manual? Would that translate into happier customers and less time spent by you putting out fires? Would that really make you unnecessary? Would you see it as a threat or a boost to your own job security? Could it possibly turn you into a hero of sorts and perhaps free you to do other things?

What supervisors need is an all-new perspective on their value to the company. The most valuable managers are those who are able to build teams that are capable of self-management, sort of pro-active downsizing through leadership efficiency.

Reason number two for not letting go: Not every employee is ready to accept empowerment. This can be a matter of training or simple psychological makeup.

Before you criticize your crew for failing to think, ask yourself what tools you have given them to support independent thinking. Employees who are unsure of your intentions or who do not believe that they really have your permission and encouragement to serve customers with abandon are not about to get creative.

Worse is the possibility that you are smothering them under a blanket of policies and procedures so thick that even those areas not specifically covered by policy are treated as though a policy exists somewhere.

Ask yourself what evidence your employees have that you would support them if they stepped out of the box—and failed. Some folks never stray out of the box of conventional thinking and strict adherence to policy because sticking to ''That's our policy'' or ''That's the way we've always done it'' is much safer. (Notice that this is particularly true for older employees who may be closer to retirement and see absolutely no self-interest in risk-taking.)

One first step to empowerment is hiring people who will, with training, willingly take risks when it comes to pleasing customers. Oh! You thought you were the one taking the risk? Not even!

When an employee is faced with an opportunity to openly defy corporate policy or even old tradition, you can bet they are thinking less about the consequences for the company and plenty about what could fall down around their shoulders. It is the employee who must be the risk-taker in a partnership with the boss, the trust-giver. This empowerment stuff can be quite a stretch for everyone!

Not everyone will accept empowerment. No matter what kind of environment you create, it's not reasonable to expect that everyone will automatically jump on the bandwagon and put customers over policy. This is the simple yet sticky matter of having some employees who just aren't interested. These folks have to go.

Sorry! Even in a market where it is tough to find qualified employees, you have to face the fact that folks who will not accept responsibility simply cannot be left in charge of anything. They are not qualified for the job you are offering.

For the vast majority of employees who are sitting on the fence considering whether or not you are serious about allowing them to make decisions, know this: They come to you with a history that probably does not support independent thinking.

We tend to complain about not being able to find trained people when the fact remains that no matter who we hire, they are trained when we get them.

New hires come to us trained to do a jillion things, most of which we would rather they not do!

In previous jobs they may have been trained that it's okay to show up late or call in sick at the last moment. They may have been trained to avoid making decisions because a mistake could bring down the wrath of the corporate gods. They may have been trained that corporate folks talk about quality and service but, when push comes to shove, it is short-term profits that count the most.

Employees who, in previous lives, were clobbered for "wasting" an overdone hot dog or granting a refund on the thirty-first day without a receipt are not about to risk stepping out of the box just because you whipped up a trendy new mission statement that tells them to put people first. No, this empowerment thing is going to take some time.

But you can do it. It's worth the effort. Your employees will love you. Your customers will thank you.

Your family will get used to having you at home.

Nine

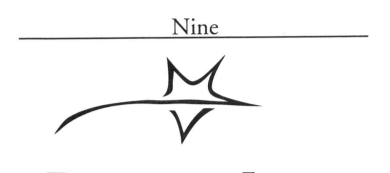

EMOTIONAL LABOR

You can relax now. I have an important point or two to make but you're going to have to read through a couple of stories before I get there. Trust me, you need the stories to fully get the point. So relax.

Sunday morning, September 1st.

It took a little longer to get started this morning. There was the dog to walk and rough; there was breakfast to be enjoyed over the Sunday paper. Of course, I made umpty-ump trips to smooch on Melanie who is working at the kitchen counter, editing what I have already written.

I fished through my notes and out jumped a story. At first I thought to save it for another project, but it wouldn't leave my hand. So read on, please.

AMERICAN PIE

Her name is Darla. She doesn't look at all like the cute little girl you remember from the Mouseketeers. Nope, this one's much rounder, forty years older, and every bit as feisty as any freckle-nosed child, mouse ears or not.

This Darla, our Darla, slings hash, huevos rancheros, and chicken-fried steak lunches at the Roundtable Cafe in Mintour, Colorado. Mintour is a railroad town: Built by the railroad and about to die by the railroad when they pull up the tracks and send the big engines and long coal trains rumbling elsewhere. Here at 10,000-plus feet, and only a few miles from chichi Vail, Mintour is an anachronism about to be run over by reality.

Most of the population has left Mintour. Even the Roundtable, a huge pivoting bridge that used to shoot railroad stock into a railroad version of a garage, is gone. Today the townsfolk clean guest rooms and serve Chardonnay to the tourists who come to ski.

Darla is a great server. Bouncing from table to table, sliding a cup of coffee on this table, dropping an order of toast on another. Darla can really dish it out.

When we slid into her booth, we expected breakfast. Instead, we got a show!

I'm a bit of a tease. In Darla, I found a match. (No wonder her granddaughter loves her so.)

The uniform of the day was a kind of lumpy Denver Broncos sweatshirt.

"Denver Broncos. Hmmm. That's some kind of sports team, isn't it? Didn't they used to play football?"

"Your friends are going to get breakfast. Where do you plan on eating today?"

"Hey, I'm sorry! I happen to be a big fan of Jim Elray, so bring me a few extra jalapenos!"

"Yeah, right! That's John Elway! You just dug yourself a little deeper, pal!"

"A little touchy since you gave up Roller Derby, aren't we?"

"The cook is a friend of mine," she threatened. "And he's just spoilin' for a fight!"

And on and on we went. Darla served everyone's breakfast, except mine. Mine she held back just long enough to tease, saying that I would have to wait until I paid proper homage to the Broncos.

Breakfast became an experience. Hot, fresh, delicious and served just the way I like it, with hot sauce and pizzazz!

Darla deposited the check with a flourish. "I brought you something special. Be sure to leave a big tip. I have my eye on another Bronco shirt over at the Wal-Mart!"

I was in the men's room when Darla came to our table to collect. Our friend John had placed a hundred dollar bill on the table.

When Darla returned with the change, she said, "Put this in your pocket and tell your friend that if he expects to see change, he'll have to deal with me!"

There are servers, waitpersons, service staff, even waitrons. Darla was none of these. She is a waitress of the old school: the sling-it-on-your-table, dish-it-out and take-it variety. A real slice of American pie.

I had a picture taken with Darla and left a big tip. (I heard there's a pretty nice Bronco shirt over at the Wal-Mart.)

A few miles and half a light-year farther to the east sits tiny Vail, Colorado. The beautiful people play there. The beautiful wanna-bes work there. I don't know who owns the shops and restaurants, but one of them needs to go looking for a few Darlas.

On a snowy preseason Saturday night, we followed the streetlights across the covered bridge, up the narrow lane, around the corner, and down the stairs to a cozy little restaurant. The snow bunnies and their honeys had tromped in for Chardonnay and pupus after a long day primping down the ski slopes.

When the server took my order, I asked for a jalapeno on the baked potato. Why not? I needed something to top off the peppers that Darla had loaded on my huevos rancheros at breakfast.

"Sorry," said the server, pointing to the menu.

Yep. There it was. Big as you please. Printed right smack on the bottom of the page—"NO SUBSTITUTIONS!"

"I don't want to substitute, just add. And all I want is a jalapeno."

"I'll try," she sighed in a breathy, ain't-life-a-bitch, "valley girl" voice.

When the food came, it looked very, well, very Vail. Lots of color, nice petite portions. Not the manly, fat-laden portions you could find at any respectable truck stop.

She placed my plate just so, saying, "The cook said, 'absolutely, no way' on that jalapeno. Sorry."

Well, sorry, my backside!

Fancy menus and haute cuisine (how do you spell haute, anyway?) do not a restaurant make. It takes Darlas. People who just enjoy being with people. Period.

DON'T WANNA BE POOR

In her own words, she was "just a secretary."

I don't believe that people are "just" anything. People, maybe, but not defined by what you do, only what you are.

I tried to make small talk, inviting her to skip her duties long enough to sit in on my seminar.

"I can't do that," she replied, looking at her feet as if in search of a reason. "I have a report to get out and if it's not finished, I may have to work over the weekend."

I asked her about the report, you know, looking for anything that might keep this fragile ego in motion. But she had little or no idea what the report was for, who saw it, or why it was a matter of life and death, only that it had to be completed just hours before the weekend.

"I bet your husband won't be happy if you have to give up a Saturday." I had noticed the wedding band and took a chance.

"Oh, he won't even notice I'm gone. He's not the kind."

"And what kind is he?"

"Well, let's just say that he won't notice. You might say

that he's not much different than my first husband. I don't make very good choices when it comes to men."

"Well, once I can understand. But twice?"

"I was getting close to forty, and, you know."

"Actually, I don't. What happens at forty?"

"At forty, if you aren't married, you probably won't marry. So I married."

"I guess you wouldn't blame it on love, would you?"

"I just didn't want to be poor another day."

A sad commentary on life's choices, wouldn't you say?

DESIREE

Occasionally I get a little bored of speaking to one audience after another. This was one of those days.

I was the scheduled speaker at a resort in Pennsylvania and decided that it might be fun to gather up a waiter's uniform and pose as a member of the staff while my audience-to-be took a break. They wouldn't know me, and it would be a fun way to get to know them without the formality artificially assigned to guest speakers.

"Desiree. That's a beautiful name."

I was just being chatty and trying to strike up a conversation with one of the real servers.

"Thank you."

"French?"

"It means, the awaited one," she blushed, just a little.

"My name is Scott. It means, he who hardly works," I kidded.

But she didn't take it as a joke. Instead she whipped around quickly and nearly demanded to know if I was telling the truth.

"No, just kidding. But why the reaction?"

"Oh, my fiancé is named Scott, and he hardly works. It sounded like you were talking about him."

"So why doesn't your Scott work?"

"I don't know. He just lays around the house all day waiting for me to come home and cook dinner."

"And you think that this will change when you get married?"

"Won't it? I mean, won't he want to get a job and buy a house and all those other things?"

"Quick quiz. Do you think about him constantly? Can you hardly wait to see him when you get home? Are you bursting with pride when he goes to see your mom? Okay. I can tell from your response that your answers are no, no, and no.

"Look, I have a kid your age so I could be your dad. Do you mind hearing from Dad for just a minute?"

"No."

"You are not in love, 'cause if you were, you would be thinking about your fellow all day. You wouldn't be able to wait until you see him at the end of the day, and you would be parading him everywhere.

"Think about your Scott and ask yourself if this is your idea of how you want to spend the next thirty or forty years; because, trust me, it isn't going to change."

She could barely look up. I knew that I had hit the mark and that it hurt. I felt sorry.

"So, why did you say yes to this guy?"

"He's the only one who asked."

"Has anyone, even your Scott, mentioned that you're a charming, attractive young woman?"

No answer.

"Well, you are. Now what are you going to do with that?"

Before she could answer, the doors to the meeting room burst open. Show time! I went to work, playing with my audience/customers as I served them sodas and fun. This is a wonderful way to get to know an audience.

When the crowd started to shuffle back to the meeting room, I raced to do my share of the cleanup before heading backstage for the introduction. A tall, charming, attractive, and now, smiling, young woman swept to my side and took my arm. She put her face close so that I couldn't miss her words.

"Thank you. I made an important decision today. Thanks, Dad!"

TWO FLOWERS

Positively Outrageous Service has often been compared to Random Acts of Kindness, an idea espoused in a book of the same name.

While in Victoria, British Columbia, Canada, on a speaking assignment, I received a phone call from Art Charleston, a meeting planner and head of Pro Speak, a speakers' bureau serving the Canadian northwest and the world.

"Do you have time for a cup of Java with me and my partner Greg?" came the voice on the phone.

"Sure! How about 10:30 in the hotel coffee shop?"

I had never met either of the two gentlemen and had little idea of what to expect. Most of our communication to date had been by fax.

I found a table in the corner of the dining room and stood looking for my guests. After a few minutes I heard happy conversation heading my way and looked up to see two friendly looking men walking straight toward me, each with a huge, beautiful bouquet of flowers. My first thought was that they were just particularly joyful delivery men about to make someone very happy.

They said, nearly in unison, "There he is!"

I looked behind me to find their target. There was no one. In an instant they were at my table introducing themselves with flowers. I felt like Miss America. The flowers and the sentiment were beautiful! What better way to surprise, delight, and totally disarm a new acquaintance?

"We teach a seminar called 'Giving to Get,'" explained Greg.

No explanation needed for this firm believer in the Law of Harvest.

"We thought you would enjoy receiving the flowers and enjoy them again when you give them away. We suggest that you give them away in your seminar this afternoon. If you do it one flower at a time, you can make quite a few people happy."

"Thanks! They're the perfect way to warm a chilly day. You can bet I'll have a good time passing them on."

I thought about the flowers and the problem that they presented. Singly, it would take forever to give them away. Besides, I preach that you should go for the big impression.

After our visit, the flowers and I went to our room to think about the keynote and consider the fate of the flowers. In addition to the Law of Harvest, I also believe, by whatever mechanism, the "way" tends to reveal itself to those willing to watch.

On the elevator down to the lobby and checkout, I said hello to a sweet elderly woman driving a snazzy red walker.

"I'm off to lunch with a friend," she crowed. "Special occasion, holidays and all," she added with a smile accented by ruby-red lipstick that hadn't been obligated to follow the lines. More accurately, it followed all of the lines.

When we reached the lobby level, the door slid open.

"Oh, dear," exclaimed the enchanting Canadian accent. "First I went too far up, now I haven't gone down far enough!"

"Ma'am, the only thing below this floor is parking and left or right doesn't seem to be an option with this elevator. This is probably your floor," I nodded toward the elevator door. Nodding was all I could do while juggling a garment bag, briefcase, and two bundles of flowers. The flowers and I got off, hoping that she might follow rather than descend into the parking garage.

She poked her head out the door but otherwise refused to budge; she was certain that she should get off but uncertain as to why. She looked as confused as the proverbial deer caught in the headlights.

A crowd began to gather at the elevator, wanting to take it back up.

"There's my friend! Down there!" my elderly friend said, her voice a half octave higher, as she scooted a little further from her perch.

"I'll get her if you would like to roll out of the elevator and let these nice folks get to their rooms."

At the bottom of about a dozen marble stairs stood another elderly woman. This one drove not a walker but a pair of the most sensible shoes I have ever seen.

"Ma'am? Your lunch date is up here!"

She turned, "hummphed" through her dentures, and began to clomp up the stairs one painfully slow step at a time.

"You're on the wrong level for lunch, and you can't get there by elevator," she announced to her friend in a way that made it clear that it was my fault.

"No problem, ladies! There's a wheelchair lift right around the corner. I'll help you get on it, and you'll be at lunch in no time. Follow me!"

I hobbled along the corridor half limping as each step banged the garment bag against my leg until I reached the lift, tossed all but the flowers aside, and pushed the call button. Behind me could be heard a swish-step sound followed by a scrape, scrape, and a clomp, clomp as my new charges made their way in unison.

I opened the lift gate, pausing in mock surprise as I pointed to a sign that said, "Caution! five-hundred-pound capacity."

"I don't know, ladies," I shook my head in mock puzzlement. "Do you think it's safe for you both to go?"

They giggled and kept on swishing, scraping, and clomping until I had them safely installed on the lift.

"Just push this button and open the gate when it stops at the bottom."

"Young man, do you work for the hotel?"

"No. I'm just a guest on my way out."

"Well, you should work for this hotel. You're very nice."

"Thank you!" I turned to pick up my things and then remembered the flowers I was still holding. "I almost forgot! You're not allowed to ride this lift unless you have flowers! Merry Christmas!"

I presented the nearest lady with a full bouquet, and both began giggling as the motor on the lift started them to the next floor. As I descended the marble steps and headed for the door, I could still hear them giggling and talking about that nice young man with the flowers.

When I arrived at my engagement, I still had one bouquet. The women behind the registration desk were delightful and made for a charming audience as I explained why I now had only one bunch of flowers. One, a cute mop-topped woman with sparkling eyes, seemed to especially enjoy the story.

"So what are you going to do with the last bunch of flowers?"

If this was a hint, I missed it entirely.

"Are you going to give them to Nan?" (Nan was the conference host.)

"Nope! Not for Nan. When the right person comes along, I'll know," I smiled. "Mind if I leave them here while I check out the room?"

"Put them close and I'll watch them," smiled Mop Top.

"I bet you will! Just don't watch them all the way to your car," I said, letting her know that she wasn't in contention.

When I returned from checking out the room, Mop Top said, "The flowers are fine. We had a few lookers but I told them they were reserved for someone special."

"And they are!"

I scooped up the flowers and presented them to Mop Top. She was thrilled with a capital T.

"You're the obvious choice. You really love flowers and it shows!"

Mop Top beamed and thanked me profusely while her friends smiled to signal agreement with my decision.

Maybe it was just one of my better days. Maybe it was the flowers. But when I left the platform that afternoon, two hundred people stood to shower me with applause and cheers, my version of flowers on a chilly day. What goes around comes around. I've always known that intuitively.

Now when I practice Positively Outrageous Service I'm tempted to duck, just in case what goes around comes around really fast!

HERE'S THE MEAT!

In case you were wondering if we would ever get to the point, this is it.

All labor is emotional labor. What separates the artist from the rest is a matter of emotion. In labor the emotional content is readily visible.

Have you ever watched an artist operate a backhoe or a forklift? There are some who simply dig dirt or pile pallets. With others, the work is a gentle ballet—motion against time and space.

I've long believed that cooking breakfast at Denny's was, for me, a combination of karate and ballet. Every movement has purpose; every thought is connected to a greater whole. I do believe that you can tell the difference.

When we ask audiences of managers to estimate how much more effort their employees could expend, or how much more productive their employees could be if they really were motivated, the average answer we get is 30 percent! How do you account for that missing third? Where did it go? Why doesn't it come to work? Because all labor is emotional labor, and folks who are not emotionally connected to the job are leaving their most valuable contribution at home.

The truly great organizations (departments, families, or teams) are emotionally charged. Last week, John Lowe came to the office to give me a physical for an insurance policy. Mr. Lowe is known locally as a tough, high school football referee. As he stuck little suction cups to various body parts, we talked football. More specifically, we talked about the emotional content of the game.

He said, "You know before the kickoff which team is going to win." My ears perked up, "You do?"

"The team that has the discipline almost always wins even if the other team has the skill and physical advantage."

From here I'll paraphrase. The team that is emotionally "present" and invested has an advantage that is almost unbeatable.

Mr. Lowe cited a contest between two local high school rivals. One of our local teams came onto the field arguing among themselves and their coaches. There was profanity and other negative language. Their opponents took the field fired up. When their coach spoke, it was always, "Yes, sir!" or "No, sir!" There was no profanity, negative talk, or dissension. However, the boys were without doubt outclassed by their bigger, more experienced opponents. Yet, as Mr. Lowe put it, "They went through the other team like Grant took Richmond."

Emotional labor may have added 30 percent to the size of the line or 30 percent to the mental acuity of the receivers. Who knows how much?

And who knows how much it could be doing for you?

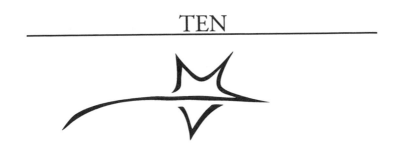

TEN

Two-Way Street to Emotional Labor

T he trick is to get employees emotionally involved. As you can see from the opening stories in the previous chapter, there are billions of folks who just want to be loved, or who are hungry to be a part of something larger than themselves.

When my dad worked for International Harvester selling farm equipment, we used to ride past other dealerships, all turning and saluting as we hummed "Hail to the Chief"! Corny? You bet! But, by golly, to this day when I see a Farmall tractor (now an antique), I want to salute.

Trash and treasures, the logo'd bags, and pens and whatnots that the meeting trades give to customers and potential customers at trade shows, are often rationed, if not forbidden, when it comes to employees. That's goofy! These are the folks who love being associated with a big-name company. And, these are the folks who are leaving their brains and hearts at home, which are the assets you most need.

In another book, *How to Get What You Want . . . From Almost Anybody,* I gave four steps for doing just that. They work equally as well at work and home as they do when you are a customer.

POS Point: You are never a customer, always a seller.

You are never a customer because the other guy always has something you want that is not included in the base price. (That is, a discount, information or an added service. More likely it is an idea or attitude.)

RECOGNIZE WHO HAS THE POWER

And it isn't you, pal. You can put your butt on your shoulder and pound your chest, saying that you are the boss, while the crew is silently thinking, "Oh, yeah?"

When it comes to the emotional portion of labor, the employee always has the option of withholding and you have no idea when it is being done. Instead, you kick the dirt and complain that "these employees today just aren't motivated" (whatever that means).

There are several ways to purchase emotional labor. First and foremost is to recognize that it exists and play to people's need to belong to something larger, stronger, and maybe better than themselves. Of course, you have to run an organization that satisfies the definition.

What goes around does indeed come around. Companies that adopt a charity as their corporate charity are doing more good for themselves than for others regardless of their motivation. When employees individually donate a few bucks, they get a "feel good" worth exactly that, a few bucks. When they are a part of a company where collectively they donate big numbers and incredible amounts of time or talent, everyone in the company gets a "feel good" as big as the whole, even if their individual contribution was small.

"We gave the XYZ group over a million bucks. Helped 3,500 disaster victims."

You get the idea.

By the way, one of the best ways to tell if you have purchased emotional labor is to listen to your employees talk. If they refer to the company as "they," as in "they have a rule that . . . ", you ain't got it.

MARKET YOURSELF

It is an awful misconception that the customer is always right, and that servers serve out of sheer love of mankind. Baloney! Servers give the best service and workers give their best work to people, organizations, and ideas that they like. Period.

If you want to get the best of your employees' time and talent, you must recruit them every day by marketing yourself to let them know that you are worthy of their best.

Take your trash and treasures to your most important customer, your employees.

When the organization takes the high road on an issue or sale, let the internal customer know that they have yet another reason to be enrolled in the cause. And cause is exactly what you must have.

Take the classic battle between Southwest Airlines and United Airlines for the lucrative California air commuter market. United has a competitor; Southwest employees have an enemy. They are not fighting for profits or ROI. Southwest employees are defending honor, the Holy Grail, and their families and livelihoods. And that's how Southwest wins anything and everything. Marketing rallies the troops, not the customers.

Imagine a company where, when under threat from the competition, the employees would spend their off time to travel to the branch under siege and volunteer to join the battle. Unbelievable? That's what Southwest Airlines' employees have done in the California air wars. Off-duty employees use personal passes to fly to California bases and help turn planes at the gate, sell tickets, answer questions, and, in general, support the "mission." That's the value of emotional labor at work.

ASK FOR WHAT YOU WANT

It's the dumbest thing. We know what we want but so often fail to communicate exactly what that is. This is as true with our bosses and employees as it is with our vendors. Who doesn't harbor at least a little disrespect for an underperforming employee? What if you went to them and talked straight? What if you said, "I need you to be here on time every day without fail. I cannot tolerate when you leave early, take long lunches, and spend time on the phone that isn't business-related."

If you'll try it, I will!

REWARD EMOTIONAL LABOR

Maybe that should read "celebrate emotional service." Emotional service is emotional! There is no sense in holding back on banners and cakes, plaques, and certificates. People want, need, and will die for symbols. What meaningful symbol would motivate you? What would motivate your team players?

Some say that what we are talking about is cheerleading. That would be correct.

Cheerleading is goofy, except when they are cheering for you.

Good partners build one another. Kahlil Gibran said that it is better to fill one another's cup than to fill a common cup. Maybe, maybe not. Maybe it is best to fill a common cup and one another's as well.

LANGUAGE OF SERVICE

Servers talk differently than others. Servers are givers. Anyone who is not a server is a taker.

Kare Anderson was here on a short visit. Kare is an expert on compelling communications, and one thing she advises is to use a you-us-me model when serving. First, what is in this for you? What is in it for us? What is in this for me?

If we use the same model to manage emotional labor, think how that might change the focus of corporate communications.

Most corporate talk is from the top and is about what "I" need, not what "you" need. It may focus on what "we" need, but that is often an imperial "we" that translates as "I."

When was the last time you asked an employee about his or her needs? If you want to benefit from the emotional portion of a team player's labor, you must meet the emotional needs that are part of the package.

We get physical labor and we pay hard currency. Okay, I brought my body here by nine o'clock and parked it in this cubicle until five, actually five of five; you paid, so now we are even.

POS Point: Emotional labor is paid for in emotional currency.

What is the emotional content of the job? How are you compensating for emotional performance, that is, for bringing the heart and soul to work along with the body that takes up space and moves on command? Maybe it's time to rethink what you are buying and how you are paying.

RISKY BUSINESS

POS is risky business, like flying or love or driving the freeway. You could crash and that is scary. But it is in the possibility of the crunch of metal or heartstrings that lies the thrill of delivering a good dose of Positively Outrageous Service to an unsuspecting soul who may need love in the worst way.

In fact, those who are most difficult to love are often among the neediest. Positively Outrageous Service has nothing to do with being deserving.

Even when you have the best of intentions, delivering POS can blow up in your face. I waded into an audience to play, approached a smiling young girl, and found myself poking a handheld mike at her slightly panicked mug. I should have known better. Good Lord, I'm supposed to be a pro. Too late to back out, I fired a simple question, expecting to play. She could barely manage a squeak in response.

I tried to encourage her and said, "Great answer! But we all want to hear it. Let 'er rip all the way from your diaphragm!"

The poor, sweet innocent crumbled in embarrassment.

The dumbest things can trip you up when you set out to love on an audience or team or market. Even a weak vocabulary can get you.

The question is this: "If POS is so darned risky, why bother?"

Because POS makes most people smile, including the giver, and that makes the potential for a "crash-and-burn" worth the effort.

True, there are those who are naturally playful, but most of us need a little coaching. We need to be taught. You can teach people to be playful. And as too much of corporate America has proven, you can also beat the play out of most anybody.

Play isn't reserved to one side of the counter or telephone or even television.

My grandpa used to hold his hand over his hearing aid, which created a whistling feedback that sounded very much like an antique radio being tuned to a faraway station. He usually saved this demonstration for those moments when the Denny's waitress was approaching our table.

"Come in, Miami. Come in, Miami," he would intone as the hearing aid warmed to an eerie wail. "Come in, Miami. Can you hear me?" he would continue as the waitress's eyes grew big as saucers.

Grandpa would then explain that he was CIA or FBI. Or

if he thought he could pull a really long leg, he would claim to be with PDQ, anything to charm the bejeebers out of just about anyone.

A lady who called to a radio show I was doing reported that her favorite opening line for those awkward moments when sales clerks seem to have difficulty seeing your corporeal self is to approach with a smile saying, "Hi! Can I help me? Would I like to buy this?"

If you are getting the idea, stand by. I'll give you plenty more ideas for creating an opening line for almost any situation. You'll discover that even for something as complicated as human nature a few pronounced rules of engagement will make the job easier. Once you know the key to writing a customer service script, you will be able to play with almost anyone at any time.

IN FUN

This POS stuff doesn't work every time. There will be moments when the "oops" is clearly your fault. Most of the time when things don't go well, it will be because you have had the sad misfortune of stumbling upon someone who is not yet what we call, "in fun," a term we use to describe those who are not psychologically ready to play.

A guy drives up to our outdoor menu board.

"Hi! May I serve you?"

"I want a two-piece mixed chicken order," he moans, then quickly and emphatically adds, "and that's all!"

Now, what do you do with someone like this? Do you attempt to play with this guy? No! You leave him alone! Unless, of course, you are a professional.

And I'm a professional! (Careful, kids. Don't try this at home!)

"Yes, sir! That's one two-piece mixed order and that's all! Drive right on through and I'll have you outta here in a New York second. And I won't even mention our sweet, juicy, buttery corn on the cob. No, sir. I'm not even gonna mention that corn on the cob. Just a two-piece mixed order and that's absolutely all. I'll have you outta here in a flash!"

As this fellow pulls up to the window, I drag an ear of corn out of the cooker and let the butter just ooze off of that puppy.

"Excuse me. What kind of corn did you say that was?"

"Oh, this corn? It's sweet, buttery, USDA, Grade A fancy, five-and-a-half inches of corn on the cob that has been cooked until it is absolutely bursting with flavor. That's what kind of corn this is."

"Well, go ahead and give me an ear."

"I'm sorry, sir. But you've driven over the I-can't-sell-you-anything-else line. I guess we can let it go this time, since you asked so nicely. But next time you're going to have to drive all the way around and get back in line!"

～∾～

Yogi Berra said, "You can see a lot of things just by looking."

Rather than a restatement of the terminally obvious, I think what the great wordsmith meant was that if you want to learn something, all you have to do is be observant. Very few of life's mysteries involve rocket science.

The best way to get good at reading books is to spend a lot of time reading books. The best way to learn to read people is to spend a lot of time reading people. And it doesn't hurt to pay attention while you are at it!

Determining whether someone is "in fun" or not is only a matter of paying attention. A guy wearing a clown nose is making a rather obvious statement. The guy is goofy and doesn't care! The rest of the world is only marginally more difficult to read. We wear our feelings on our sleeves, rather than wearing noses.

Just look and it will be as plain as day how a customer is feeling. Turn your fun volume up or down to match the circumstance. Sometimes you'll need to turn fun off completely and let compassion or seriousness rule for awhile. The important point is that great servers match the tone of the served.

STOCKING

Long story, nice ending. Please read on.

From first class, with the wide leather seats and endless supply of Chardonnay, flying is an entirely different experience when compared to riding in the back of the bus. I don't mind riding in the back. Heck, I'm a skinny guy and fit nicely in the coach seats.

But there is one nice, not-so-nice thing about first class. Riding up front is quieter. Perched far from the whine of the engines and close to the wine in the galley, the world in first seems built for introspection.

I was doing just that on American Airlines' flight 1006 from San Antonio to Philadelphia one Christmas season. It was the year that Melanie and I started a tradition of giving up presents for one another and sending the savings to a local charity. For two people in their middle years overburdened by "stuff," the idea of anonymously providing Christmas for our less fortunate neighbors was the best gift of all.

The challenge comes in that we continue to hang our stockings on the mantle and wait for a Santa with a much limited budget. Twenty bucks, that's all we can spend. And the goal is to stuff the stocking with surprises that delight an otherwise spoiled "Yuppie" couple.

As the plane winged smoothly into the darkness, I decided that a poem would fit nicely in my sweetie's stocking. I wrote:

Just a little something
in the bottom of your stocking
hanging from the mantle
on Christmas morn.

A scribbled line,
a note of passion,
leaping from a love
that can't be torn.

To know your smile . . .
the greatest present,
your laugh, your tears
are mine forever.

When times were tough
or days were pleasant,
a crowd of two
just us together.

So comes this note
in the bottom of your stocking . . .

I was stuck. I needed an ending but none was in sight.

So, I looked out the window to see the moonlight reflecting off a cloud base a few thousand feet below and my own reflection in the yellow reading light over my seat.

A soft voice said, "Would you care for some candy?"

I was startled just a bit. It was the flight attendant, a cheerful woman who had quickly learned that water was my favorite drink after Chardonnay.

"No," I responded before thinking to add, "but I know someone who will enjoy it."

She smiled and dropped a small gold foil box on my tray table. The neat, black lettering proclaimed, GODIVA. Small world. Just as I had been lost in thought, looking for an end to my silly poem, an ending found me.

GODIVA chocolates are my sweetie's favorite. I had bought her GODIVA for our wedding day twenty years earlier. So I wrote:

So comes this note
in the bottom of your stocking
hanging from the mantle
in our warm home.

And in the box
you may find chocolate
rich as the love
that we have known.

Just a little something
in the bottom of your stocking
hanging from the mantle
on Christmas morn.

I couldn't resist calling the flight attendant over and telling her the story of our Christmas tradition, the poem, and how she had inadvertently supplied not only the perfect chocolates but a perfect ending as well.

Although she stood in the shadow of the darkened cabin, did I only imagine a tear?

"Ladies and gentlemen, the captain has turned on the seat belt sign signaling our approach into the Philadelphia area. Please discontinue the use of any electronic devices, stow any carry-on that you may have brought out, and . . ."

I must have heard that monologue a gajillion times. I could recite it in my sleep and probably have. So I turned to the task of buttoning up and returning my "seat back and tray table to its upright and locked position" before hearing the announcement that I knew would follow.

A gentle hand touched my shoulder. A paper bag was passed to me.

"I know you can afford a much better bottle of champagne. Knowing how your limit is $20, I thought I would help you fill that stocking. Merry Christmas!"

And Merry Christmas to you—and to all who know that the most precious gift of all is serving others.

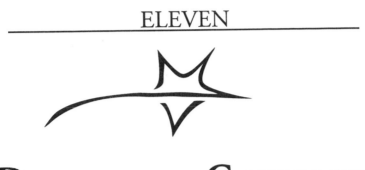

ELEVEN

DEVELOPING CUSTOMER EYES

What's the difference between the amateur and the pro? Give up? It's the details. Pros handle the little stuff. Amateurs do not. There is a popular saying on T-shirts: "Don't sweat the small stuff—and it's all small stuff."

Okay. I give you that the professional also has an endearing quality of never getting rattled. The amateur panics, overwhelmed by details. In the restaurant biz, we would say, "He's in the weeds," or "He's snowed under," meaning that someone was hopelessly in over his head. So maybe the T-shirt should really read: "Don't panic, but watch the details."

Holly Stiel, a favorite customer service expert, is fond of saying, "You never get bitten by an elephant. It's the mosquitoes that eat you alive."

On one hand we're saying that the professional is a master of details; on the other hand we are advising not to let the details eat you alive. Maybe that's why service in high-pressure situations seems to require a very special personality; someone who watches over every detail, no matter how minute, yet has the ability to remain calm in the middle of chaos.

CHAOS BUILDS CHARACTER

Watch a pro handle a crisis situation and you will see something special. The pro doesn't even attempt to handle a zillion things at once. The pro has an uncanny ability to handle a zillion things, one at a time. This is actually a three-step process.

First, the pro is able to look into the very face of chaos and pick out the first thing. You've heard the saying, "First things, first." When a pro steps into a crisis, he or she picks out the "first thing," handles it, and picks out the next "first thing." Experience helps the pro pick out the most important "first thing"; but, picking the most important "first thing" is not as important as choosing somewhere to get started.

I remember my dad walking into a busy coffee shop kitchen and finding me totally buried. His tactic would be to find two clean towels and a couple of milkshakes. He would toss one towel to me and nod that I should stop everything and wipe down the work area. He would start restocking the prep table, and then we would squat behind the grill and chug our milkshakes. Dad would then line up all the order tickets, and we would start working on the "first thing." Once that was accomplished, we would take the next "first thing." And soon there would be a pass-through window full of hot, fresh dinners waiting to be picked up by the servers.

That lesson has served me well ever since. Writing a book is a matter of picking the "first thing," doing it, and starting on the next "first thing." In fact, there isn't a project anywhere that is more than a series of first things.

Pros have the ability to look at chaos and pick not "the" first thing, just "a" first thing.

THE SECOND THING

Pros at any job have the ability to decide not just what is important. They also have the ability to see in a heartbeat those things that don't need to be done at all. As a manager trainee years ago, I was behind the building carefully painting the knob on the electricity shutoff switch. You know, that handle on the side of a commercial building's breaker box that acts as a master shutoff for power into the building. I was using a small artist's brush to apply bright red enamel to the end of the handle.

I thought I was really doing something. T. Scott Gross, master of details. I knew that the "brass" would visit my store and be, oh, so impressed that I had handled every last detail right down to painting the handle on the breaker box.

As I was taking an imaginary bow, one of the brass hats that I wanted to impress paid me a surprise visit. I jumped half out of my skin when he rounded the corner. Before I could even say a weak, "Hello," he said, "That looks great! I've been to a lot of our stores and have never seen the handle on the breaker box painted before."

I started to glow, thinking, "Scott Gross, you are one brilliant guy who is definitely on the way to bigger and better things."

"How much product do you think this bright red handle will sell?" he asked with a smile as wide as Texas.

"Well, I uh . . ."

"By the way, I was driving by and thought I'd better stop and tell you that your pole sign isn't on. From the road this place looks like it's closed." He started to walk away when he suddenly turned and added, "Oh, yeah, one more small thing. Your employees must have decided to go on break. When I walked in, there was no one in sight to wait on me."

"Gross, you are a real numb nuts," was all I could think, as I stuffed the paint brush into a paper towel and started for the front.

To seal the deal, Mr. Brass Hat called to me as he slipped into his car. "The knob looks great! Maybe we can use your idea systemwide!"

The real pro knows what is the first "first thing" and does

it. And the best of the best will quickly recognize the last "first thing" and not waste a second thought or an ounce of resources to handle it. They will let it die while they attend to things that really matter.

NONSENSE

There is another characteristic that marks a pro as different from the amateur. That is the ability to see more "first things."

Think of any industry from healthcare to hardware. Notice there is not a single vendor in that entire industry that doesn't provide the basic products or services of the industry. For example, is there any barber who does not cut hair, any dry cleaner who does not clean clothes, any restaurateur who does not serve food? The answer is a big, fat "NO!"

Everyone in any industry meets the basic needs of the customer. Period.

What, then, is the difference between the best in the business and the also-rans? Is it the big stuff? Nope. It's the details. Little, itty-bitty differences that add up to make big differences.

In the Olympics, what separates gold winners from bronze winners? Does one run the entire race while the other walks? The difference is in the details. Small, nearly unnoticeable differences in technique and training that are only observable at the finish line.

The same is true in your business. The leaders are those who sweat the small stuff. More important, the leaders are those who know *which* small stuff to sweat when they see it; then they do something about it.

CONTACT!

12:18 P.M.: Surveillance systems at New York Telephone's network Guardian Center report a central office battery discharge, followed by a fire alarm a minute later.

The World Trade Center has been bombed, which is a story that you and half of the human population know well. What you don't know is how a fast-acting, highly empowered team of dedicated NYNEX professionals helped put the pieces back together again in record time.

12:25 P.M.: Evacuation was well under way.

12:30 P.M.: Twelve short minutes after the first alarm, a NYNEX initial response team passes some of the thousands of smoke-blackened evacuees as they pour down the fire stairs to safety. The team is headed in the opposite direction. They're going in.

Doug Mello, then NYNEX group vice president, Manhattan, would be the man on the spot, literally, continuously for the next ten days and for uncounted weeks to follow.

Deep in the hollows of the World Trade Center, two massive telephone-switching units stood near-silent sentry, quietly making the millions of switches necessary to move voice and data on a scale too awesome to comprehend. They are high-tech. They inhale electric power. When the power is cut, they run on batteries. And very well, thank you, just not for long.

Within a few minutes, Mello had organized the advance team of technical experts to visit the switching center at the stricken World Trade Center. In hindsight, it may seem like an odd place to have such a major communications hub, but that's where the customers are.

The "techies" reported back with frightening news. The battery backup that is designed to handle temporary power outages was not likely to last for the duration of the problem. To Mello, that meant that communications for the hundreds or even thousands of people still trapped in their high-rise offices would, or could, soon be cut.

There was an alternative, but one that was fraught with risk. The redundant features of the system could be taken off line to conserve power. The good news was that if the plan worked, an additional few hours of grace would be earned before the system involuntarily shut down. The gamble came in the fact that any additional difficulty would send the system into irreversible overload and shut it down completely.

Mello and team played the odds and prayed in the margin. The system held. It held long enough for a team of specialists from AT&T and Northern Telecom to arrive and inform them that the disaster had not been abated, but merely pacified for the moment. If the batteries ran out before power was fully restored, the system would shut down so hard that the damage would require a minumum of two days to repair.

The team had been monitoring call volume. Over twelve hundred calls per hour were still being made by panicked survivors to worried friends and relatives. The two switches in the basement had become more than a hulking infrastructure; they were lifelines to the world. We'll wait.

7:25 P.M.: Seven hours and what seemed like a lifetime after the blast. The NYNEX team was walking on eggshells, hoping the batteries would last.

Suddenly the lights flickered, then burned steadily. Not a breath was taken. Would they hold? Was this simply a cruel tease? Had power been restored?

With no more than five minutes of battery power left, the system was saved.

The end of the crisis marked the beginning of a whole new feeling of enthusiasm and camaraderie. Team players who had gambled together and come up with the big one found themselves with new viewpoints about what it meant to be part of a winning team.

Now the real work had to begin.

Mello called upon his colleagues from other departments who would need to work as an extended team and asked if they would give him the right to serve as their quarterback. They quickly agreed to rally their individual troops to report for duty.

Every salesperson was called to work and ordered to contact every customer. This job started at midnight Friday and continued into the wee hours of the morning as customers were rousted happily from their beds to talk about how to relocate their business communications services. Some were easily call forwarded. Others were scheduled for emergency installation of all new service. Some were even relocated to a NYNEX office building and given desks and office space.

Every day, NYNEX took out full-page ads to explain what progress had been made and to offer its services to anyone who had not yet been contacted.

At first, conference calls among team players took place twice each day, at noon and at six in the evening. The first few calls took upward of thirty minutes, soon shrinking to less than five minutes.

"People got used to working solo. We got a grip on the five or six things that we really needed to know. People got good at giving very clear glimpses of the situation," said Mello.

The extraordinary teamwork caused Mello to think, "If we can do these extraordinary things under such extreme conditions, why can't we do this every day?"

~⌒∾⌒~

The truth is we can do extraordinary things on an ordinary basis. How? Well, as Mello and team demonstrated, the pros see all the small stuff. They don't sweat it. They handle it! Sweating the small stuff is misplaced energy.

I probably speak to a hundred audiences every year. What do you suppose scares me the most? Facing a thousand people with high expectations of being entertained while they are learning or the prospect that there will be a thousand people and three thousand seats?

It's the small stuff that gets you. The mosquito, not the elephant. I can handle an audience of a thousand. No sweat. In fact, the more the merrier. But the thought of trying to be funny in a room where people are spread all over the place gives me the willies.

When I go to speak, I want to know that the lights will

be right so the audience will be able to pick me out of the background. I want to know that the sound system will work and that there is a backup mike. I want to know that my presentation doesn't begin with an open bar. I want to know that there won't be any waitstaff in the room to distract when I get to the power line of my best story.

And I couldn't care less if there is room-temperature, lemon-flavored water at the lectern or fruit waiting in my hotel room. That's amateur night. The small stuff is the real big stuff and the big stuff is the only stuff that matters.

Amateurs cannot tell what is big stuff and what is simply stuff. Worse, amateurs sometimes can't recognize stuff when they see, smell, hear, touch, or taste it. Pros are master sniffers. They use all their senses to contact the environment and take control of the details.

Sit in a restaurant with a longtime hospitality pro. Don't bother trying to eat. Your company will be like a cat in a roomful of rocking chairs, listening to every plate and hum, sensing, and connecting with the environment as if hot-wired to the building and everything inside. The amateur won't catch a thing, but the pro might suddenly excuse himself saying, "There's something going on with the exhaust fan. It sounds like it may be out of balance. I bet they didn't clean it last night. Let me check."

Real pros are plugged into their environment. Like a hunter who sees every upturned leaf and twig, or like the mother who hears every whimper and sigh of her newborn in the next room, pros intuitively know when to react and when to ignore.

Good managers have great operational awareness. They coach their team players until they are skillful. To get people interested in handling the details, they have to be shown the beauty in the details. Great managers teach awareness so that team players know when and where to put those skills to work.

THE CONFIDENCE OF DETAIL

Attention to details inspires great confidence. What do you think when a mechanic keeps the work area spotless? What do you think when a mechanic keeps himself spotless?

Whenever we need electrical work, we call Benno. Benno can work all day in the blazing, south Texas sun and still look like a professional. I have never seen him show up on a job with junk tossed in the back of his truck. Public carelessness promises equally careless work. You just know that Benno will do good work simply from his appearance and the appearance of his tools. He goes about things in a very organized, workmanlike manner that inspires confidence.

When we arrive early to check out a room prior to an engagement, I relax the instant that I see that the A/V group has also arrived early, having carefully installed every cable and light even for a small job. It makes me feel good when I see someone taking care of the details.

The other day we were at dinner with our son and "daughterette," my Kiddo and his Sweetie. The waitress raced over to gush about how much she was enjoying the new car stereo that our son had sold her and installed at his store.

"Is it working perfectly?" he asked.

"It's won-der-ful!" she smiled. "The only thing is that if you crank it all the way up, and I know you shouldn't do that, it sometimes will cut out for just a second."

"Maybe so," was Rodney's response. "But that isn't the sign of a perfect installation. I know exactly what it needs, and if you will bring it in, I will have it fixed and out of there in less than fifteen minutes."

Details. That's why my kiddo is killing 'em in Kerrville. And if you are watching the details, your customers are watching you and feeling confident.

My favorite group of detail watchers are air traffic controllers. These men and women miss nothing. And at 200 miles an hour, a little miss can mean a lot.

The other night we flew into San Antonio from Fort Worth to drop off my brother Steve. It was pitch dark and rainy with the clouds dropping lower and lower as we neared the San Antonio control area. When we were passed to San Antonio's approach control, I felt an instant sense of relief.

One of the San Antonio controllers has rented the voice of James Earl Jones. When this deep, rich, evenly paced voice slides in through the headset, you feel like you are hearing your orders direct from God. "Fly this way, little Mooney. Okay. Easy does it. Now swing around and join the ILS to one-two. Attaboy." (Controllers never talk like that.) The tone is always cool, measured, and professional. Flying in the dark, even when you can't see the runway or anything other than black, black, black, you still feel confident that you are not about to tangle with a granite cloud because they are so good about the details.

Details. You have to notice the details.

What are you doing to make your customers feel confident that you have the details in hand and give them equal value to the big stuff?

HELL-OOOO!

Have you ever wondered how it is possible that an employee can walk right by a mess or totally fail to catch a customer with an obvious problem?

In a very fine hotel, we were surprised when a friend joined us for lunch. She walked right past the dining room hostess saying, "I'm looking to meet my friends for lunch."

Our friend found us sitting at a table for two so I pulled up a chair from a nearby table. We were within 20 feet of the hostess who was standing quietly waiting for the next guests to show, watching us get settled. We waited for a server to bring water, a place setting, and a menu. When this didn't happen, I went to a nearby table, removed one of the settings, and placed it in front of our friend. I then went to the service stand for a pitcher of water.

All the while, the hostess watched. Her job is seating not serving. At least that is the way she sees things. She may have even been wondering why the server had not jumped immediately to the task. When I turned toward her to pick up a menu, a small light must have turned on.

"Oh! Your friend is having lunch," she said as I reached past her to pick up a menu.

"You figured it out! Good!"

Are clerks and servers stupid? Lazy? Dumber-than-a-box-of -rocks?

Not even. They just haven't learned how to see through the eyes of a customer, and that's the fault of management.

Hire someone from a household where dishes are routinely left dirty in the sink or where beds are not made each morning, and I'll show you someone who is hardly likely to notice sloppy housekeeping at work. Why would you notice at work something that is normal in your home?

I know many managers who make a point of walking potential employees to their car so they can see how the prospect treats their own property and space.

Developing "customer eyes" is a matter of training, either at home by their environment or at work by the boss who has a vested interest in both his internal and external customers.

For more T. Scott Gross . . . www.tscottgross.com

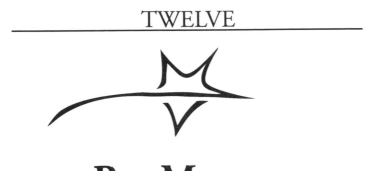

TWELVE

BIG MOUTH

Below the desk, it's socks and underwear. Hey! It's 9:15 P.M., it's my office, and I'll dress the way I want! Above the desk, it's a black felt hat, which feels kind of expensive. It has a broad brim that hangs low with a white silk band and three cuffs, or pleats. Very cool. Very forties. I feel like Elliot Ness, but the guy who gave it to me is more likely related to Al Capone.

Above the desk, maybe above the neck, I look like the one and only Al DiLiberto. I'm wearing the hat for inspiration. Al gave me the hat today when we stopped at his Boccone's Restaurant, Deli, and Music Emporium. It's quite a place. If ever I wanted to bet on seeing Positively Outrageous Service in action, I'd bet on Boccone's. Actually, I'd bet on Al DiLiberto.

Melanie, who at forty-six still looks awfully cute to me, and Kare Anderson, a world expert on cross promotion, joined me in my trek to Al's place. Once in a while you have to have Italian food, and in my book, Boccone's is one of the few places where food is art and service is magic.

I knew that I would find a service story at Boccone's, so I took the little tape recorder and an extra pen in case the Mont Blanc rolled over and died. Well, I got the story. See if you can beat me to the punch line.

We weren't 3 feet inside the door when Al spotted us and started bear hugging just so we would notice. He hadn't met Kare before, but she got hugged, too. I got the feeling that if the guy driving the beer truck had walked by at the moment, he would have been included in the hugging. If that's the Italian way, count me in.

Kare is a noticer, an observer. One of the first things she noticed was a poster that featured a particular brand of canned tomatoes. Don't ask me why Al elected to put up a framed photo of canned tomatoes. He just did, that's all. The entire restaurant is plastered with photos and paintings and stories. Only Al can tell them all.

"I notice you feature . . ." Kare mentioned the brand of tomatoes. Al immediately turned and insisted that there was no way you would find that brand in his restaurant.

"They add citric acid," he said, immediately launching into a doctoral dissertation on canned tomatoes. "It helps them cook the darned things. But tomatoes don't need more citric acid. You want the sugars and only the natural ones."

About here I lost the story because Al had dragged us into the kitchen to prove a point.

Any kitchen staff caught in his wake was sucked along on a stream of requests, call them orders, that sent them scurrying. There was English, Spanish, and a torrent of Italian all mixed in the milieu of dishes being washed, exhaust hoods exhausting, and Al, squinting from beneath a black hat just like mine.

Spoons appeared from thin air, a can of tomatoes was produced from nowhere, and in the next instant, the great tomato lecture continued. The can was opened and four spoons were dipped.

"Taste this! Taste this!" (Yes, there are tomato missionaries.)

I admit. The tomatoes were good. No, they were great. Almost a sauce in themselves. "As sweet as summer," I caught myself murmuring in the din of a busy kitchen.

"I heard that," shouted Al. He shouts even when he doesn't. It has something to do with Sicily he once explained. I forgot how Sicily came to be blamed for Al DiLiberto's penchant for volume, but take my word for Al's word. Somehow, Sicily is at fault.

"Taste this!" The lid on a forty-gallon, steam-jacketed cooker popped open, and more spoons were produced. We did. Good Lord, that stuff was delicious. Someone from heaven was cooking a batch of . . . I don't know. It was red like the canned tomatoes with a spicy flavor that was the far side of wonderful—some kind of Italian something that Al figured proved his point about the canned tomatoes.

When the lid banged shut, I began looking around for my service story and didn't see a thing. No worry. Al never disappoints.

We sat for a late lunch. Wanna see Al? Don't bother going at the peak times. He will be busy. Lots of hugging to do, food to oversee, servers to serve. That's just Al. He knows who rings the register, and it's not some writer from the Hill Country who only stops to steal a story every book or so.

Al ordered. Until you have seen this sideshow, you have no idea what it means to have Al order. In a matter of minutes, enough fabulous food appears to feed a Third World country. When Patti asked for my drink order, I asked her to bring tea, half of whatever Al ordered, and a family of four to assist with the tidal wave of lunch that was about to break over my belt.

The conversation continued. First it was the olive oil. Then the steam-baked bread. Al turned food into art and service into a passion. I still waited for the service story.

I checked the men's room. Al has this thing about restrooms, says they should be so clean, there could be no doubt about the kitchen. He has them cleaned (or repainted) every fifteen minutes. I mean those things are immaculate.

But that's not a service story—although I should mention that Al runs one TV spot that features a man coming out of the restroom saying, "Those are the cleanest restrooms I've ever seen!" Imagine that. A clean restroom as a competitive advantage.

Actually, it was Al's radio commercials that made me want to meet this guy. I asked a friend for the introduction and ended up spending the most wonderful evening with Al and his alter ego, Mary Helen (his wife and partner, in all senses of the word). They say that beauty is only skin deep and that ugly goes clear to the bone. Maybe. But odds will get you that Mary Helen is beautiful all the way through.

Al and Mary Helen were running the original Boccone's and doing all right. Then he started the radio spots and created first an explosion followed by what seems to be a restaurant empire. Customers were so intrigued by this brusque guy who seemed so softly human behind a New York Italian accent that they just had to come to Boccone's to see the real thing.

When they showed up, they fell in love with Al and Mary Helen and stayed long enough to find out that the food was better than first-rate. It is nothing short of wonderful. The little business boomed and exploded, finally moving a few miles up the road to bigger quarters and even bigger ideas.

Al kept taunting the public to try his authentic Italian hospitality from his bully pulpit on the radio. Writing his own copy and delivering the message daily at about noon, Al talks about food, service, and even life as it should be lived.

Like the Taster's Choice coffee commercials, Al's listeners became fans, waiting eagerly to hear what he would tell them next.

It's a good thing Al has honest intentions. People will do almost anything for Al.

And maybe here is the service story.

As lunch unfolded, we talked about his latest commercials. (We live just far enough into the hills that we rarely catch Al on the radio.)

"The one that got the most response was one I did about kids and work. When we hire young people, we almost have to become their mom and dad. They have no idea about work. We have a long orientation training that includes two hours just on ethics."

"Two hours on ethics?" I had worked for years in the corporate world and couldn't remember ever hearing the word mentioned much less discussed. "Two hours?"

"Yeah. Two hours. And, honestly, that sometimes isn't enough."

I tried to take notes but there was no way to keep up. I did get the part where Al told about teaching new employees that if they want to be a manager, they have to begin by behaving like a manager. That if they want to get ahead, the first step was not to ask for a promotion but to do the things that would earn them a promotion.

It was sort of the old be-do-have lesson that we preached in our home while my kiddo was growing up. (He got the message by the way!) The idea is that if you want to have the things that managers have, you don't start by wishing you had manager things. You start by being more, well, managerial, whatever that means. Then you do the things that managers do and, eventually, you will have their "things" (i.e., the power, the pay, and the responsibilities that managers have).

Al produced a list of statements that are key to the ethics training at Boccone's. Statements like:

- Don't ask for entitlements.
- Understand the laws of life.
- Don't blame someone else for your life.

He presents a list of excuses and then dares anyone to use them. Around Al, never say, "That's not my department," "I forgot," "No one told me to go ahead," or "That's the way we've always done it." I'm certain the training includes both exhortation and empowerment to be quality fanatics.

Al pointed to a sign over the door that gave the two cardinal rules he borrowed from Richard Mayberry. I wrote them as he repeated them: "Always do what you agree to do"; and, "Never encroach on others or their property."

"You have to have a lot of love and caring, but every once in a while you have to kick butt. But you can't get angry. There is no such thing as good, righteous anger. When you start to punish an organization, you are in trouble. When you start to install video cameras so that people don't steal, you are in trouble. When you make the rules so rigid that people can't move, you are in trouble.

"I'm allowed to make mistakes and grow. I have to do the same with our team. That's kind of what leadership is about, seeing the potential in difficult situations."

I asked about one of Al's radio ripostes that deals with just the issue of effort, responsibility and ethics and Al promised a copy.

It's pure Al.

Hello everybody! This is Al DiLiberto, owner of Boccone's Italian Restaurant, with a few questions for you young people out there. When was the last time you did some work around the house to help out your parents? If you're like most families these days, both parents are working to make ends meet. Are you helping them, without being asked, in those little ways that can make their lives easier? When was the last time you put away the dishes, cleaned up the garage or the bathroom, baby-sat your little sister, or washed your own clothes? Do you know how to polish a pair of shoes, press a shirt, or mend a hole in a sock? Can you name three general uses for bleach? Do you know how to make mashed potatoes from scratch? In other words, are you getting ready to be a grown up by learning how to work, or are you taking your parents for granted? If you are spending more than an hour a day in front of the TV, or haven't read a book cover to cover in the last month, chances are you are cheating yourself. Face the facts, your generation, in general, will not have as much financially as your parents. How will you survive? The time to set good work habits is now because good habits develop the character needed to survive in a tough environment. You have to do something about it! Come to Boccone's and see how we work. You can work and be successful, too!

I've got a dollar that says this one sold more pasta than any other commercial he has ever done.

Al told me that he heard from people everywhere, even from out of state, and all were positive.

I have long held that every business has a personality. Good product. Great location. Fair prices and clever marketing, that all helps. But it is the personality of the business that shapes both expectation and experience.

Important. But not the point.

Kare sat at attention as Al told stories about growing up Italian and about strength of character. He paid homage to those immigrant heroes who came before him to pave the way. I think he honors his family every day by creating his own opportunity.

When it was time to take Kare to the airport, an incredible sandwich appeared, wrapped to go along with a box of fresh-baked pastries bound to make the seat next to Kare the lucky spot on the plane.

Still no story. Well, lots of little stories. Stories about quality, marketing, ethics, and training. But no service story, and I'm writing a service book.

"Did you notice how the employees jumped when Al marched us through the kitchen?" This was Kare's contribution as we raced along Highway 1604, hoping to make her flight.

"And even though he was giving lots of orders, it was

pretty clear that they really like and respect him," she continued.

Kare notices those kinds of things.

And therein lies the story. Sort of.

"I think it may be the other way around," I guessed. "They don't like him in spite of his insistence on doing things the very best way. My bet is that they love him because he insists on such high standards."

If this is too subtle, then read it again.

In a world where good enough is, well, . . . good enough, a man for whom excellence is the only way kind of stands out. If you were to work for someone, who would it be? Someone who settles for okay, or someone who won't even tolerate second best?

It is my experience that the most loved bosses are not the pushover, easy types. The ones who earn your love, first earn your respect. Everyone wants to be associated with a winning team, and no team ever finished first by settling for second.

The best way to build and keep a team of winners is to insist on being the best. Even if we are talking about the cleanest men's room in town. Given the choice of where you might work and for whom you might work, maybe there is some attraction to working where the restrooms are clean; so clean that you can feel good about having a part in cleaning them. So clean that you feel clean.

And if that's not an important service story, then I don't know what is.

It's ten o'clock. I'll take the hat off now. Good night.

THIRTEEN

THINGS SERVERS HAVE TO KNOW

If you want to tick off a customer, the easiest way to do it is to serve customers out of order. This seems to be a no-brainer; but, try this as a test. You are about to serve a customer when the telephone rings. Which customer is first in line? Is the customer who calls on the phone in line at all? The answer is (drumroll, please) the customer at the counter is first!

Answer the telephone, but tell the caller that there is another customer ahead of them. Offer to take their number and call them when their turn comes up. If they say they only need to ask a simple question, ask the customer at the counter if you may have their permission to handle a quick question. If the quick question turns into something complicated, excuse yourself and promise to return the call as soon as possible.

TRANSFER

One of the worst offenses in customer service is transferring a caller to an unanswered line. Whenever you transfer a call, it is your responsibility to remain on the line until the call is answered. At the very least, watch the hold light on the line to make sure that someone picks up.

NEW LINE

When you have to open a new register or serving line, the worst thing you can say is, "I can help someone over here." This does nothing but create anxiety. Some customers will hesitate while they decide if they should move from the line they are in. By the time they make their decision, it's too late. They stand and seethe in anger as someone who only a moment ago was standing in line behind them is now getting served ahead of them.

You could say, "I'll take the next in line." This is a pretty good approach but often there is some debate as to who really is "next in line." The best approach? Walk over to the person who is next in line and say, "If you'd like to step over to the other register, I can help you next!"

LOOK, THEN THINK!

Last week I took my 83-year-old grandmother to dinner. Gran is pretty spry but uses a cane "just in case." The hostess asked how many were in our party and our smoking preferences. We said, "Three. Nonsmoking, please."

She said, predictably, "Walk this way." Well, if I could walk that way, I'd probably apply for the job!

Where do you think Miss Observant sat us? At the table farthest from the door!

Look, then think. Always! Of course, everyone wants to be seated close, but little old ladies with canes should be given extra consideration, or at least offered the choice of immediate seating or waiting for a table a little closer to the door.

WAIT A MINUTE!

It really doesn't matter how long customers have to wait. It only matters how they feel about waiting.

If you have dialed 911, a ten-second wait can seem like an eternity. Imagine if you ordered an elegant dinner or a custom-made suit and it was delivered in ten minutes. You might be a little suspicious! In fact, if there was no wait at all, you might begin to doubt the specialness of the meal, suit or whatever.

Heads-up customer service experts pay attention to the wait. They make the waiting area pleasant. They may offer something to read, drink, or do to make the wait seem shorter, or at least less of a drag.

Really smart service folks make the wait a part of the experience. I know of a theater chain that installed windows between the lobby and the projection booth so that patrons waiting to be seated for their movie can watch how the film is handled. Another great example is theme parks where they let the long lines leading to the attraction snake through specially designed areas that give those waiting in line something to see.

In cases where a customer is waiting at home, a clever way of handling the wait might be to call or write from time to time advising on the progress of their order. People don't mind waiting as much as they hate being ignored or forgotten.

As we speak, or write, I'm waiting on the new office furniture we ordered in Dallas. It sure would be nice to know what progress has been made. Maybe if they sent me a note, a picture, or something the wait wouldn't seem so looong! (My vibrations must travel! In the mail today was a postcard of a joyful toddler with a handwritten thought balloon that said, "Really? It's almost ready!" That Elizabeth is very sharp!)

If you are clever, you might figure a way to make waiting so much fun that your customers would actually rather stand in line!

What can you do to make waiting part of the experience?

I'M NOT INVISIBLE!

Next to the wait, customers hate to be ignored. When you ignore someone, you are telling them that they are not important. The solution is simple. Look up, smile, and let the customer know that you know that they are there. You could even say, "Hello! I'll be right with you." Always acknowledge waiting customers.

SEVEN MINUTES

If I hurried, I could make it. There was just enough time to wolf down a quick breakfast and race to catch an early flight.

Armed with a *USA Today,* I left the room and homed in on the hotel restaurant.

It was exactly 7:00 A.M. when I straight-armed one of the two French doors to the coffee shop. Pow! (Why do people have double doors if they are going to leave one in the eternally locked position?)

I hit the other door and was served up the same punishment (only this time to the other elbow).

I checked my watch, 7:00 on the dot. Oh, well. It was a cheap watch. Hardly Naval Observatory time. I waited, shifting impatiently from one leg to the other.

At 7:02 I pecked on the window to attract the attention of one of the employees lounging at a nearby booth. The hostess looked up.

I tapped on my watch and mouthed in exaggerated lip-sync, "SEVEN?"

She tapped her watch and mouthed back a big, fat "N-O" as she shook her head from side as in "no way."

Two minutes later, I tapped and mimed again.

Same response.

A few minutes later we went through our ritual. We were well into a relationship when she looked at the cash register and decided to unlock the door. By then I was hotter than the grits on the buffet.

"Excuse me for being impatient. I know this is a cheap watch, but gee whiz, it's not off by seven minutes."

"It's the dumbest thing," she said as she sighed the sigh

of a low-level employee who must endure dumbheaded boss decisions and the wrath of customers on a regular basis. "Our computer is seven minutes slow. We open seven minutes late every day."

"Did you ever consider . . ."

"Setting the clock?" she finished my sentence. "Can't. Only the field rep can touch the computer, and he's never here when we aren't open. Do you know what is just as dumb?"

I didn't really want to know. I wanted breakfast and out. But I was going to hear anyway.

"We stay open seven minutes after closing every night."

Sigh.

Here's to all of us who are left to wither under the glare of systems more suited for timing lawn sprinklers than for running our lives.

IT'S ME!

There is no sound as sweet as the sound of our own name. The same is true for your customers. Whenever possible, call your customers by name.

And how do you learn a customer's name? Easy! Just ask! "Hi! I see you in here all the time. My name is Bill." Then stick out your paw and be prepared to make a friend. Pay careful attention to hear exactly how your customer responds. If she says, "Hello, Bill. My name is Mrs. Smith," she doesn't want to be called Janet or Sally or whatever. Until further notice, it's Mrs. Smith.

If you want to be less direct, read their name off their check or credit card. Maybe they are wearing a uniform or a name badge. Maybe you will overhear someone in their party call them by name.

One client enters all the customers' license plate numbers in the computer. When a customer pulls onto the lot, the license number goes into the computer and out comes the name of the customer and what they purchased on their last visit. It's pretty impressive to walk into a store and be called by name after an absence that may be months.

I'd bet a dollar that's how the folks at Men's Wearhouse do it. Not long ago I walked into their store and was greeted by the same salesman who had waited on me months earlier.

"Good morning, Mr. Gross. How have you enjoyed the wool sport coat you bought last fall?"

Pretty impressive!

Even when you know how it's done, it's still pretty neat to walk into a store and be called by your name.

How could you use technology, high tech or low tech, to dazzle your customers and call them by name?

P.S. Men's Wearhouse, please call for your dollar. I stopped in for another suit and the salesman called me by name again. And, guess what? No computer. Just sharp salespeople!

THIMK!

That's not a typo. It's a point!

The other night we went out to dinner and decided to share a salad. Since we were with guests, we were sitting on opposite sides of the table.

We were careful to tell our server that we would be sharing the salad.

He brought a beautiful salad, heaped high on the plate, plenty for two to share especially since we both ordered entrées. One problem: one plate!

All that is required for great customer service is for us to pay attention. Great servers are great noticers. They notice the small details. They anticipate problems and fix them before the customer is even aware that there is a problem. Great servers are problem-solvers.

DON'T TELL ME, JUST SAY YES!

"That comes with coleslaw, sir."

"I understand. But I don't want coleslaw, I want a baked potato."

"Sir, it comes with coleslaw."

"I don't think you understand. I don't want coleslaw. I do want a baked potato. I do not expect to eat for free. I am willing to pay whatever is reasonable to have this meal served the way I want as opposed to the way your chef thinks it should be eaten."

I don't get it. Why do so many businesses insist on serving things their way? Why can't I have it my way?

When I was two years old, I pulled the Christmas tree over—lights, ornaments, and all. My dad raced for the basement, soon returning with a large nail and a length of wire, intending to nail the darned thing to the wall. But my grandfather (and he was really grand!) said, "Ted, that's his Christmas tree. If he likes it better on its side, just leave it alone."

If a customer is willing to pay for it and wait for it, just say, "Yes!"

POS Point: Look for ways to say "yes" to your customers. How could you customize and personalize your product or service?

ORIGINAL SIN

Few ever think of it this way, but waiting to be served is often a matter of paying for someone else's sins.

Take, for example, the backlog we have in our court system. Let's say that a particular court has a backlog of cases that is three months long. If the court is hearing cases at about the same rate as they are being filed, the backlog will remain three months, theoretically, forever!

One case is discharged as another is filed, always the backlog will be the same.

How in the world did the court get three months behind in the first place? It could have been an extraordinarily long case. Or perhaps the judge was ill for three months. No matter who or what was the original sin, every plaintiff, or customer, to follow will pay again for that original sin by suffering through that same three-month wait.

It's not a matter of one person waiting three months. It's every person thereafter who must also wait three months.

This same principle applies to any situation where people must wait. Mess up on one customer and, as long as you are serving customers at the same rate at which they are arriving, every customer who follows must wait all over again.

Anything can set a perpetual wait in motion. Maybe you run out of product for a few minutes. Maybe the power goes out. It could be anything. What you must realize is that as long as customers are being served as fast as they are arriving, it is impossible for a line to form. But, once a line has formed, unless customers can be served at a rate faster than they are arriving, that line will persist forever—original sin!

Imagine that you take your VCR in for repair and are told that it will be three weeks. Do you really think that it will take three whole weeks to fix the thing? If you do, better buy a new one because three weeks of labor charges will far exceed the price of a new one.

The chances are your VCR will be fixed in an hour or two. For the remainder of the three weeks, it will be "standing in line," paying for some original sin too old to be remembered.

Sometime, when the repair shop was first opened, there was no line or wait at all.

"Bring it right in," they would tell their customers by phone. "We'll get right on it. In fact, if you want to wait a few minutes, we can probably fix it right away."

Then Fred, Joe, or whoever, decided to take a little vacation and, poof, original sin!

POS Point: Do you have customers who are paying for an original sin?

MELANIE'S FURIOUS!

I walked into the kitchen to ask MG what are her biggest customer service peeves. She said, "I have one from just a few minutes ago! I told the people at the credit union that we did not receive our statement for last month. They said that it was sent, and they had not received it back from the post office. And, if I wanted another copy, the charge would be two dollars!"

"What I really heard is they're telling me that they could not have made a mistake, that the post office didn't make a mistake, and that I must have misplaced it and should be charged for making them work to create another copy! I can't believe they think I'm that stupid!" This gal was furious!

Instead of apologizing for not getting our statement to us, they have decided to charge us two bucks to set things right. Now it's not the two bucks that are at issue. It is the principle that matters. And Melanie will have the final word.

"I'm moving our savings account and business account down to Jeff's bank in Comfort," she smiled.

"Is that dumb or what? Losing a good account over two bucks. Instead of accepting responsibility for getting the statement to me, they tried to make me responsible for not receiving what they supposedly sent."

POS Point: What dumbheaded rules do you have that may be putting customers in second place? Better said, what rules do you have that may be sending customers to some other place?

HOT POTATO

Your job is to solve problems brought to you by customers. It is not to protect the company, occupy space, give sage advice, or stock shelves. It is to solve problems. And, to put it bluntly, if you aren't solving problems, you are a problem.

Think for just a moment about your place of business. No doubt most of the folks there are pretty customer-focused. They have a "whatever it takes" attitude and generally pull together to get the job done, whatever it is. On the other hand, dollars to donuts you have at least someone on the payroll who hasn't quite got the message. This is the person who always talks about the organization as "they," as in, "they expect me to do too much," or "they have weird policies."

The folks who are real team players always talk about the group in terms of *we*. We have to work together, or we can do this if we try.

The player who talks about the group in terms of *they* is the most likely player to be the problem rather than the solution.

They players have only one goal: self-promotion. They want to be excused from the rules; they want to be paid first and then perform. Most important, or dangerous, *they* players are more likely to pass a problem than to fix it.

This could be as simple a matter as walking past a piece of trash in the parking lot. If a *they* player makes it to a management position, you get the impression that Lincoln had returned and changes his mind on the slavery issue! A *they* player will walk past a spill or mess saying, "I'll send someone to take care of this!"

We were speaking at a large resort hotel when the general manager decided to join us as we walked the property to get a little exercise and fresh air. Directly in my path was a paper wrapper that had blown onto the property from gosh knows where. Instinctively, I picked it up. The GM looked at me kinda funny but said nothing.

A few steps further was another wrapper. Now this was a rather expensive property. Beautifully landscaped, gorgeous. Not the kind of place where a single thing was left less than perfect. The GM stepped over the wrapper.

I was just a half step behind, so I bent quickly and scooped up the second wrapper. The GM looked at me as if I had landed from another planet, took the wrappers from my hand, and tossed them back to the ground!

"Don't worry. I'll send someone out to take care of this," he smiled—a classic *they* person.

By the way, that GM is no longer a GM. He is unemployed. I hope he finds good honest work picking up trash!

The job of anyone is to solve problems.

Your job might be to solve the problem of dirty dishes, or the problem of infection. You may be a solver of hair or parking problems or political or domestic problems. But if you live and breathe, Problems 'R' Us!

As a problem-solver you should know that unsolved problems are what keep you employed.

NEVER SEND A CUSTOMER AWAY WITHOUT A SOLUTION

We're working on a training program for fixed base operations (FBOs), service stations for airplanes. At FBOs the level of customer service far exceeds that of a traditional service station. Taxi to an FBO and you can expect someone to guide you to a parking space on the ramp. They will chock the wheels, tie down the plane if necessary, place a carpet on the ramp for you to step onto, and immediately ask if you need fuel, transportation, catering, or other services.

Let's imagine that you are working reception at an FBO and a customer mentions that there seems to be a problem with the number one navigation receiver. Your FBO does not service avionics (most do not), but there is an avionics repair center on the other side of the airfield. What do you do?

(A) Say nothing as your company does not service avionics.

(B) Tell the customer that there is an avionics center on

the other side of the field, and tell them where to find the pay phone.

(C) Give the customer a card from the avionics center.

(D) Offer to place the call for the guest and, if needed, offer to have the plane moved to the repair station.

The answer? It's D, of course! We never leave a customer without a solution.

What if you are running a manufacturing operation? You have the product prepared per the specs and delivered on time. But at the last minute, your customer says that he needs assistance with installation, which is not a service that you are staffed to provide. What do you do?

(A) Tell the customer that installation is not your responsibility.

(B) Offer to call until you can find someone who is competent and available.

(C) Suggest that the customer call installers listed in the Yellow Pages.

Okay. You know the answer. But, do the other players on the team? The job of management is to provide team players with the training they need to solve customer problems. And that goes far beyond simple task training. Team players have to know up front that their job is to solve customer problems.

When a customer has a problem, never send them away without a solution.

There may be times when a customer has a problem that is beyond your ability or authority to solve. In those cases, pass the baton but not the buck. Instead of saying, "That's not my job" say, "I'll find someone who can help you." Under no circumstance should a team player be permitted to pass the problem without another team player formally accepting responsibility for the next step.

In the situation mentioned above about the FBO, it

might be entirely appropriate for the lineman to handle getting the plane moved across the field. But the receptionist shouldn't say, "Ask the guy on the ramp to take your plane to the maintenance hangar." Never!

The proper handling is to say, "I'll have the lineman move your plane." Only when you see the lineman nodding his head has the responsibility passed out of your hands.

Too often we hear customer servers say they will check on something and we know (and they know) that the ball has just been not dropped but totally abandoned.

POS Point: Never send a customer away without a solution.

I'M BUYING YOU!

When a customer makes a purchase of any kind, included in the price is service. Sometimes we buy things knowing that there isn't much service included. Things like bulk paper towels purchased at a discount warehouse store do not include much service. However, there is some service implied in any purchase. For example, the warehouse store may not offer carryout service; but, with really heavy purchases, you can expect some assistance. Of course, clean restrooms, well-lighted parking, safe aisles, and friendly cashiers should be included with any purchase.

There is one other thing that comes with everything you sell—you. Customers have a right to expect that you would not sell a product that was dangerous if used as intended. They have a right to expect that whatever you sell will work as advertised. Beyond these expectations, customers have a right to expect that you will look out for their interests by not selling something that is inappropriate for their needs.

For the short time when my son worked for an auto dealer, he was appalled to discover that the salespeople were only interested in making sales, not customers.

"Dad, you won't believe how they operate!" he lamented after his first day on the job. "They don't care if the car they sell is right for the customer. I saw them sell a two-seat sports car to a couple who were expecting a child! And it's going to be their family car! Does this make sense?"

We often remind our video clients that included in the price is our expertise in producing video-based training and marketing programs. When they ask us for something that is not appropriate for their needs, we feel obligated to say so. After all, they're not hiring us to carry our equipment. They are hiring us to know how to use it to its full advantage. Not telling a customer when they have asked for something that is not best for them is also wrong for you!

POS Point: Customers should expect to get your knowledge and expertise as part of the package. If you withhold expertise, you are stealing.

Now, if a customer rejects your expertise, you are excused. There have been a number of times when we have told speaking and video clients that we will deliver as ordered, but that we will not put our logo on the product. By the way, when we agree to deliver, but refuse to put our name on the product, that is usually all it takes to get the client to reconsider!

For more T. Scott Gross . . . www.tscottgross.com

FOURTEEN

OPENING LINES

I f Dorothy had been in need of a way to POS, the Wizard would have said, "My dear, you already know the way to POS. You have to have a good heart, and you already have that."

Then he would have noticed Dorothy's look of disappointment and added, "But to make it easy for that good heart of yours to touch others, I have just the thing."

At this, he would have rummaged through his bag of wizardly widgets and produced with great flourish a book that looks like this chapter. In gold leaf, his version would be titled, "Rules of Engagement."

You see, most of us instinctively know how and when to deliver POS, but in the cynicism of our world, it is easy to forget the POS way. What we need is a gentle reminder. We need the rules of engagement; we need a few opening lines.

When I tell you, you won't believe that you hadn't already thought of it. When it first struck me, it was one of those moments that Tom Peters refers to as a "blinding flash of the obvious."

The actual moment I recall very clearly. I was having a late spring dinner with the executives of a major gated attraction (a theme park). I was scheduled to speak to several thousand of their employees to, you know, get them motivated about "loving on" customers, one of those things that always looks best on paper.

The complaint that came with dinner, and it wasn't a new one, was that in spite of all their training, contests, mystery shopper programs, and a dozen other permutations of "carrot-and-stick," the employees, although pleasant, didn't seem to get the hang of playing with the park guests. They gave good service, sometimes gracious service, but rarely the kind of fun, engaging service that makes customers say WOW! There is a big difference between responding to customers' needs and reaching out to involve them in their own service experience.

"We call them cast members, send them to wardrobe, give them costumes instead of uniforms, and tell them that they are 'on stage.' And, they still rarely are more than just friendly."

This lament was coming from the chief of operations of one of America's premier gated attractions, a park that has a reputation for service excellence that gives the fabled Disney folks a real run for their money. Still, there was an element missing from the service experience. Of course, there followed the usual grousing about the difficulty of attracting, hiring, and retaining good employees. Hey, this is a seasonal business, hardly a career opportunity for most.

I had the answer. It came to me in a Tom Peters's flash.

"Well, of course, they aren't going to play with the guests! They may have been to wardrobe. They may be wearing a costume, and you may have told them that they are 'on stage.' But, for goodness sake, did you give them any lines? These employees need a script! You followed the entire theater-entertainment business analogy right up to the moment when you pat them on the backside and tell them to 'break a leg,' but you didn't give them the script. You didn't even fully describe their part or character!"

There was a pregnant pause while furtive glances were

beamed around the table. No one really wanted to hear some yahoo from Texas define in less than sixty seconds the solution that had eluded them for years. Here they were with millions invested in a world-class facility, and more millions invested in marketing and promotional expertise. Add in a few assorted millions in the finest management talent available in the entire world and someone, no, several someones, had missed the obvious. They hired actors and sent them off without a script!

What we are asking people in the service industry to do is to establish a near-intimate relationship with total strangers. This relationship lasts only seconds and has little lingering value to either party other than that it holds the possibility of brightening the day just a bit (for one more than the other).

This same relationship, or potential relationship, also comes equipped with all the possibility for embarrassment and rejection we experienced as schoolchildren on the first day of school or when trying to impress that little redhead who sat across from us in English class.

Essentially, what we are asking people in service to do is to flirt. Plain, old simple-yet-difficult flirting.

You remember. You were sitting in English class and finally screwed up your courage to say hello to the redhead. Maybe you winked; you waited for a reaction. Maybe you winked again. But this time, when there was no reaction, you backed away from your move by saying, "Gee, I've been having trouble with this contact!"

Well, that's exactly what we are asking service folks to do two or three hundred times each day! And, for most folks, that is too darned intimidating!

Think for a moment about your first day on the job. My guess is that the first day on the job is right up there with the last day on a job when it comes to being stressful. In some respects, for more people than you can imagine, playing with customers, total strangers, is roughly equivalent to making every day a first day.

It's a part of our folklore that what Americans fear

most—more than large dogs, more than a trip to the dentist—is the thought of speaking in public. Yet we are hiring people by the thousands to do what? Speak in public! And it scares the living daylights out of them.

There are plenty of ways to make dealing with customers easier. First, we have to get over the idea that "loving on" customers is a matter of genetics. I contend that the problem is really more a matter of social skills, which can be taught. Of course, you have to start with folks who are at least willing to learn. Beyond willingness, little more is needed than skillful, patient coaching.

Notice for a moment that when people are given a mask their personality changes. Think about the last time you went to a masquerade party. Remember how surprising it was to discover how the normally mild-mannered folks often were able to reveal a totally unexpected facet of their personalities?

When I had a real job, Halloween was a big deal. Everyone dressed for the occasion. What surprised me were the folks in the accounting and management information systems (computer) departments who really went all out for the day. I recall one very shy young woman coming to work dressed in a leather outfit complete with spike heels and heavy chains. This is not the stuff that you would expect to find in just any closet. This was heavy-duty whip-and-chain material being worn by a woman that, in business dress, was so quiet that you had to look to see if she was in the room! There she stood, making Elvira look like the last of the Republicans.

Masks reveal as much as they hide. They also make the point that inside most of us are children willing and waiting to play given half an excuse. And play is exactly what work should be. Hard play sometimes, but play nonetheless. Yesterday someone told me that the average two-year-old laughs several hundred times each day, and that by the time we reach forty that number drops to under fifteen. Amazing! Tragic, but amazing.

Costumes, especially those with masks, are open invitations to let your unrevealed inner self come out and play. When folks are wearing a mask, particularly when the mask connotes a well-defined character, even the shyest seem capable of creating opening lines. Even the shyest can join the fun, maybe even create it.

We were having breakfast in a wonderful St. Louis hotel when I decided I needed extra milk for my cereal. I looked around, noticed Dave clearing a nearby table, and quietly called to him.

"Excuse me, Dave?"

"Dave" kept right on clearing, lost in his own world of china and silver.

"Dave!" I called just a bit sharper, not wanting to disturb the entire restaurant.

Still no sign of life from Dave. Then it hit me. That wasn't the real Dave. Servers and clerks get so tired of being clobbered by rude customers and guests that they often wear a tag with a name other than their own. I could have called for "Dave" all day and "Dave" wouldn't have answered because, in more ways than one, good old "Dave" just wasn't there!

Perhaps the best disguise of all is great training coupled with permission to play, knowing that if you accidentally step on a customer's sensitivities, you won't be crucified for your attempt to contact the terminally dead.

POS Point: Nothing gives permission like a good example.

Phil Romano, founder of half of the truly innovative restaurant concepts in America, is known for hiring drama students as servers. He stacks the deck by hiring people who are predisposed to playing make-believe. He then brings in a drama coach to teach his actors how to play the role of the world's greatest server.

Does it work? Have dinner at the nearest Macaroni Grill and let me know what you think.

~∞~

Since masks are rarely either practical or appropriate, better work on those opening lines.

One important value of opening lines is that they grant permission to play. Think about it. When have you seen an employee manual that comes flat out and tells the employee that playing with the customer is more than tolerated, it's actually encouraged?

Even if you put up a giant sign that says, "Go! Play with your customers!" who would believe it? Most workplaces are so dreary, so oppressive, that few would believe it. Think about it. Can you imagine the people you have worked for in the past actually playing with the customers? It would be easier, and probably more fun, to imagine them wearing silk boxers printed with red fire trucks!

POS Point: Offices are not for leaders. It is hard to lead from behind a desk.

Managers should always choose to work in a position where they are a highly visible standard.

Part of the problem is that the boss too often also needs help with opening lines. This makes it tough to serve as an example. Beyond the permission of a great example, read on to learn how to create a shining repertoire of great opening lines.

Remember, opening lines are a simple matter of recognizing visual and verbal cues and responding to those cues in a way that engages the customer, often in a playful manner.

ANNND . . . CUE!

Pay attention here. The best opening lines are impromptu; but, once you get the hang of this, you will discover that a few will develop that work especially well for your business. These are the ones that new employees will latch onto first. They can use borrowed lines, no harm or foul, until they feel comfortable to try a few zingers of their own.

Beware! Playing with customers is risky business. Here's a scene from our drive-through at our restaurant a few years ago:

Me: "Thanks for choosing Church's. Order whenever you are ready!"

Lady: "I'm sooo hungry! What size chicken orders do you have?"

Me: "Are you in luck or what? We just happen to have a new, one-hundred-piece "Crowd pleaser" box. How many of those would you like?"

Lady: "That's too big! It's just me."

Me: "No problem. For the larger appetite, we have a sixteen piece, a twelve piece, and an eight piece. Sound good?"

Lady: "That's too big, too!"

Me: "No problem. We have a three piece, a two piece, and a one piece. And if that one piece is too big, I can take a bite out of it and adjust it for size!"

She drove off.

This playful stuff is risky business!

A few years ago I happened to be talking to Colleen Barrett, the moving force behind the fabled Southwest Airlines. I asked Colleen if she felt that all the playfulness that is the trademark of Southwest Airlines ever creates any undesired side effects.

Colleen said that at that moment she had on her desk a letter from a woman complaining that she "doesn't think it appropriate to have her safety in the hands of a twenty-two-year-old girl in hot pants," and that she "would never fly Southwest Airlines again."

I know Colleen. A single unhappy customer becomes a personal issue with Colleen.

"I know this bothers you," I said, fishing for more comment.

"The only saving grace is that for every one we lose, we win a hundred more," answered Colleen.

Are you willing to risk a good customer against the potential for a hundred who have yet to darken the door? If you are not, you are not ready for Positively Outrageous Service. It's risky business.

Are you willing to risk being seen as a little too far out, a little too forward? If not, forget it. And forget having employees willing to skate on the thin ice of the unconventional.

For me, if a server or clerk hasn't a sense of humor, what do I care? Life's too short.

A horse walked into a bar and sat by a beautiful woman. When she noticed the horse sitting next to her, she looked up and, trying to be friendly said, "So why the long face?"

I love that! I love that! Lighten up! It's a joke!

One evening, in Phoenix, we had the pleasure of wonderful company for dinner. The summer evening was warm but not uncomfortable, and we were in the mood for good food and even better conversation. "Good evening," came a monotone voice from over my shoulder. "My name is Mark, and I'll be serving you this evening."

"Nice to meet you, Mark. I'm Gladys Knight and these are the Pips. We'll be your guests for the duration." Lurch did not get it, but I had hopes that he was just a slow learner. "Our evening special is excellent. It was featured on television just yesterday."

"So it's at least a day old. Is that why you're pushing it?"

Now, Lurch was looking over his shoulder in hopes that he would find a more civilized group. Sorry, pal. Some of us are just in the mood.

"Sir," he replied firmly, "the special is prepared to order. It is absolutely fresh."

Not everyone is in the mood to play. That applies to customers and servers, owners and the newly employed. Your job in life is not to see whom you can irritate but to discover who is ready to play and offer them a chance to join the parade.

True, there are moments when play is just not in order.

One evening I stopped at our little restaurant to "love on" the crew and have a bite of dinner if business allowed. I noticed one of the crew members closing a box of fried chicken. Something didn't look right.

"Excuse me. Would you mind opening that box?"

Christian opened the box to reveal, in heavy red lettering, these few words: Merry Christmas, Mrs. Rogers.

"What's this?"

"Mrs. Rogers called in her order tonight and sounded kind of depressed. I thought I would do a little something to cheer her up."

By the time I found a few minutes to eat, Mrs. Rogers's order had made it to her home. Pillsbury, our delivery guy—if you ever saw him, you'd understand in a heartbeat how he earned the moniker Pillsbury—said, "Mrs. Rogers, do you mind if I open this box to make certain that I have the right order?"

"No problem, Pillsbury."

Pillsbury opened the box. When Mrs. Rogers saw the message, tears formed at the edges of her tired eyes.

"Ma'am? Do you mind if I use your phone to check on my schedule?"

"Go right ahead, dear," said the now smiling, little old lady.

When the phone rang, Christian was first to answer, anxious to hear if his message had worked its intended magic. In an instant, everything stopped in the store. We were all called to the phone—management, employees, even customers—

where we tuned up and sang into the phone a rousing chorus of "We Wish You a Merry Christmas!"

That's playfulness of the best kind and one of my favorite stories. Of course, it would have been a better story had it not happened at Easter, but you get the point!

There are at least five varieties of cues that, if you watch for them, will trigger an opportunity to play.

FIVE CUE VARIETIES

1. Clothing. Pay special attention to insignia on hats or shirts. Watch for uniforms, weather gear or sports uniforms.

Color. Is it very bright or unusual?

Bulk. Is the clothing so bulky that you can barely see the person inside?

Logo or affinity messages. Read 'em and play! They tell you in plain letters the interests of the person underneath. They are an open invitation to start a conversation. In fact, starting a conversation is the reason why the wearer chose them. So, speak up. You've been invited!

Combination or item missing. Are they wearing one shoe, a tux jacket with shorts or perhaps deliberately mismatched colors?

Style. Jazzy styles are like T-shirts with printed messages. They shout "Notice me! I'm dressed for something special." It's just fine to notice!

2. Speech. Verbal cues are easy to spot. You can pick these up over the telephone. Listen for a saggy voice, holiday greeting, or other interesting way the phone may be answered. If the voice indicates the person is undecided or frightened, respond appropriately. Asking for directions is a conversation starter all of its own. Listening is the way to pick up the vast majority of opening lines. Especially listen for the opportunity to play against words that can be interpreted in a variety of ways.

> **Accent.** I like this one because it's so easy to play with. Choose an accent that is a complete mismatch and offer your "expert" guess.
> **Word choice.** Colloquialisms are invitations to play. "He was rode hard and put up wet!" is just an example of the funny ways we use language. (This one means that he was really tired and overworked just in case you live on the backside of the Mason-Dixon, meaning, you're a Yankee!)
> **Volume.** Laryngitis? Just whisper back, honey, and play a little bit!

3. Purchases. Look for signs that there is a party or special occasion in the works. Picnics or large gatherings always are a reason to talk. This cue challenges your creativity and can be a lot of fun.

> **Project indicator.** Purchase of a plumber's friend (plunger) and rubber boots. "Oh! I see you're going swimming!" See? Isn't this easy?
> **Quantity.** Purchase of one package of hot dogs and three cases of beer. "Good thing you remembered dinner!"
> **Quality.** Purchase of three killer steaks, a bottle of fine wine, and roses. "This is going to be a v-e-r-y special evening!"
> **Choice verification.** Purchaser shows his Sam's Club card as a source of ID. "I see you have a Texas passport."

4. Physical. Look for the obvious.

> **Medical.** An arm in a sling and a "Help! I've Fallen" T-shirt is an absolute no-brainer!

Cosmetic. Purple hair or exotic painted nails? Easy!

Kids in tow. Anything you say about the kiddo being cute or smart works. Be careful about saying that it looks like the person holding it!

Vehicle type or condition. Envy or sympathy, your choice! "Love that car!"

Sign on vehicle. Bumper stickers or magnetic or painted business signs can trigger a comment.

Accompanying party. Lots of options here!

5. Time. Use your watch, calendar, or newspaper to spark your creativity.

Time of day. If very early or very late, play Mom or Dad: "Hey! It's midnight. Do you know where your parents are?"

Product arrival, readiness, or availability. It's always best to lighten up for this occasion. You might need an icebreaker. "We were going to make you wait another month, but, here it is!"

Special events. Pick up on holidays, birthdays, news events, or even tax day!

TEN FREE-STYLE FORMS

In addition to the five cue varieties, there are at least ten free-style forms of humor or conversation.

Personal. Easy and best. Remember my name, and use it!

Chitchat. Comment on the obvious.

The direct hit. This is humor, straight on!

The dodge. Something ordinary said out of context.

The twist. Inferring the unexpected.

The assumption. Assume the unusual.

The double. Two meanings in one context.

The bargain. Do this for me, and I'll . . .

The exaggeration. Texans do this naturally.

The slapstick. Fun with words, situations, and funny
   product names.

Enough, already, let's put this stuff to work!

Back up several pages to the top of the list of Five Cue
Varieties and I'll show you how each might be put to use.
First, I'll complete one, then you'll get a chance to try your
hand. If at first you don't do well, it's fine to be totally intimi-
dated! We have sixteen-year-old high school kids who can do
it with style! (The numbered asterisks relate to my suggestions,
which can be found at the end of this chapter.)

1. Clothing Cues

Color: (A customer comes in wearing a Day-Glo orange
tie) "Nice tie! How many batteries does it take?"

(A customer is wearing a very bright suit)

*1. You say:

Bulk: (A customer is wearing several layers of clothes on
a very cold day) "Be careful! If you fall down and start
rolling . . . !"

(Customer has on a raincoat, hat, and boots, and is
carrying an umbrella)

*2. You say:

Logo or affinity message: (A customer is wearing a Chicago Bulls' shirt) "Hmmm. Chicago Bulls. Dennis Rod-
man. You don't happen to be looking for hair color are
you?"

(A customer is wearing a shirt that says, "If you can
read this, you're too close!")

*3. You say:

Combination or item missing: (Customer is wearing a wonderful suit but no tie) "I see you couldn't quite bring yourself to wear the tie!"

(Customer wearing shorts and a jacket)

*4. You say:

Style: (Customer wearing western clothes) "Okay. Where's the horse?"

(Customer wearing a very fashionable suit)

*5. You say:

2. Speech Cues

Accent: (A customer with a very thick southern accent) "England! I can tell you're from England. I'd know that accent anywhere!"

(Customer with a decidedly foreign accent you don't recognize)

*6. You say:

Word choice: (Secretary says, "He's tied up in his office at the moment") "Well, if you have to tie him up, I guess the office is the best place!"

(Customer asks for a whatchamacallit)

*7. You say:

Volume: (Group of diners ordering, speaking very loudly) "HELLO! COULD YOU SPEAK A LITTLE LOUDER? THAT WAY I WON'T HAVE TO WRITE YOUR ORDER, THEY CAN LISTEN FROM THE KITCHEN!"

(Customer speaking very softly, almost a whisper)

*8. You say:

3. Purchase Cues

Project indicator: (Customer purchases a hammer, nails, and small saw) "What time is the surgery? I'm an attorney!"

(Customer purchases beer, sodas, chips, dip, and motor oil)

*9. You say:

Quantity: (Customer purchases three bulk packs of toilet paper) "I hope you have more than one bathroom!"

(Customer purchases a dozen identical pairs of socks)

*10. You say:

Quality: (Customer purchases very fine sweater for someone of the opposite sex) "Someone must be very special!"

(Customer purchases most expensive paint in stock)

*11. You say:

Choice verification: (Customer purchases a set of tools) "You'll be glad you bought the entire set. I have a set and couldn't live without it!"

(Customer orders the dinner special, "Mom's Meatloaf")

*12. You say:

4. Physical Cues

Medical (Be careful!): (Customer with very bright sunburn) "Looks like you ordered medium rare and got well done!"

(Customer with arm in a sling)

*13. You say:

Cosmetic: (Customer with sports team logo carved into his haircut) "Better let me sell you a hat. Those guys didn't look too hot last night!"

(Regular customer with totally different and very attractive haircut)

*14. You say:

Kids in tow: (Customer with eight kids, obviously a day-care worker) "WOW! Your husband must be really proud!"

(Dad pushing twin-stroller; mom holding hands of two others)

*15. You say:

Vehicle type or condition: (Customer in a loud vehicle at fast-food restaurant) "Hi! When you get through mixing that batch of concrete, shut her down and tell me what you'd like for lunch!"

(Overall-clad customer in a beat up, red pickup truck)

*16. You say:

Sign on vehicle: (Customer's car has this bumper sticker: "Visualize World Peace") "For now, let's visualize lunch."

(Customer driving a bread or bakery truck)

*17. You say:

Accompanying party: (About a dozen people pile out of a van and come into store) "For a minute, I thought your car was one of those that you see in the circus—you just kept on coming! Now I realize that this isn't the circus, you must be the Mormon Tubercular Choir!"

(Group of middle-age men come in, dressed in hunting gear)

*18. You say:

5. Time Cues

Time of day: (Customer enters as you are unlocking the door) "Where have you been? I've been waiting for you!"

(Customer enters at closing)

*19. You say:

Product arrival, readiness, or availability: (Customer arrives as order is being unloaded at the dock) "You must be psychic! Your order is just coming off the truck!"

(Customer orders French bread, which is fresh from the oven)

*20. You say:

Special events: (Customer arrives as you are serving cake, and it's not your birthday) "Guess what? It's not my birthday, but we wanted cake anyway!"

(Customer arrives looking cheerful even though it's April 15th)

*21. You say:

Now for the ten free-style forms.

Personal: Use their name. (Regular customer enters) "Why, you're here almost as often as I am. I'm Joe, and you're . . . ?"

(Customer wearing name tag)

*22. You say:

Chitchat: A comment on the obvious. (Customer wearing obviously new jacket) "That is gorgeous! Where did you find something so pretty?"

(Supplier calls with information that you need; has very bad cold)

*23. You say:

Direct hit: Gentle humor, straight on. (Customer wearing a team shirt) "Oh, I've heard of them! That's some kind of football team, isn't it?"

(Customer pushes his car onto your lot)

*24. You say:

The dodge: Something ordinary said out of context. (You are about to walk out into a snowstorm) "Gotta go! Time to work on my tan!"

(Airplane passenger struggling to stow a very large, heavy bag)

*25. You say:

The twist: Inference of the unexpected. (Customer orders large drink, an apple pie, and French fries) "I see you finally got that diet started!"

(Customer orders most expensive item, doesn't flinch at the price)

*26. You say:

(Waiter wearing very fancy uniform, looks like he's a ship's captain)

*27. You say:

Assumption: Unusual assumption. (Young couple arrive, speaking to the woman) "I see you've brought your father along today!"

(To the clerk, alone in the store)

*28. You say:

The double: Two meanings, one context. (Customer in a fried chicken franchise asks, "Do you have wings?") "Ma'am, if I had wings, I wouldn't be working here!"

(Customer requests your best deal)

*29. You say:

The bargain: Do this for me, and I'll. . . . (You need special handling for a rush order) "If you'll do this for me, I'll have the person of your choice kiss you on the lips!"

(You need to cash a large check)

*30. You say:

The exaggeration: (Customer asks if new product is big enough to handle . . .) "Ma'am, this new model is so fast, it will lift the print right off your sales contract!"

(Customer asks if portion is enough to feed family of four)

*31. You say:

The slapstick: Fun with words and situations. (Server asks what you would like to drink. You are very thirsty) Waving arms in huge circles, "I'd like a teeny, tiny, baby glass of water, please. If you want, you can set a pitcher on the table, or even run the garden hose over here. Got the picture?"

(Customer walks in wearing a clown nose)

*32. You say:

"ASK THE PRO" RESPONSES

*1. Does it come with matching sunglasses?"
*2. "We have special ark parking around back."
*3. "Could you step a little closer? I'm having trouble reading that shirt!"
*4. "Have you always had trouble making those big decisions?"
*5. "That is beautiful, just beautiful!"
*6. "I love your accent! Where do you call home?"
*7. "Would that be a large whatchamacallit or can we substitute a thingamajig?"
*8. (whispered) "Why are we whispering?"
*9. "You might want to rethink that menu!"
*10. "This takes the guesswork out of laundry!"
*11. "Good decision! In the long run, this should save you a bundle!"
*12. "Mom is going to be so pleased!"
*13. "Looks like the Roller Derby will have to live without you for a while!"

*14. "I used to wear my hair just like that. (Show bald spots.) Look what happened!"

*15. "Thinking about your own baseball team, huh?"

*16. "My cousin Bubba used to own one just like that!"

*17. "You guys must be rolling in the dough!"

*18. "Sorry, guys, we don't sell deer meat. You'll have to think of another excuse!"

*19. "We were going to close early, but then we remembered that you hadn't been in!"

*20. "This stuff is sooo good, you'll want to smoosh it all over your face!"

*21. "You're smiling. It's April 15th. You must work for the IRS!"

*22. "Is your name really Angela or have you borrowed someone else's name tag?"

*23. "You sound awful, but you look marvelous. And it's better to look marvelous than to feel marvelous!"

*24. "Let me guess. The warranty expired yesterday!"

*25. "I guess you didn't bother locking the door at home. Couldn't be much left to steal!"

*26. "My Uncle Jed used to say that for a dollar more you can go first class. He died broke, but he sure was happy!"

*27. "Where did you park your boat?"

*28. "What did you do to run everyone off?"

*29. "Our best deal is out of the office right now!"

*30. "Trust me. If this check bounces, I won't even mention your name!"

*31. "You can feed four normal, hungry people, eighteen high school girls on their first dates, or invite Roseanne over for an appetizer!"

*32. Don't say a word. It will make them nuts!

Here are some fun lines that fit almost any occasion:

"Good to see you again!" (Especially nice if it's unlikely you've ever met!)

"Where have you been? I've been waiting for you!" (I use this one when the person who has the middle seat in my row on the airplane finally arrives. It always breaks the ice.)

"Thanks for calling! We need the sales!"

"If you'll tell Fred I called, you can take the rest of the day off!"

Okay, so *The Tonight Show* writers don't need to worry about job security. So what? You don't have to be Jay Leno—just you. Good, old friendly Y-O-U. Besides, customers are so surprised when anyone takes time to play with them that simply making the attempt warms their day. Yours, too!

FIFTEEN

POS STORIES

We had no sooner touched wheels to the runway when we spotted a favorite client, Kate from Play It Again Sports (PIAS). Close in tow was Steve, a PIAS franchisee in the Detroit area who was about to star in a training video that we had been hired to shoot.

There are plenty of reasons why we like working with Kate, not the least of which is that she is a consummate host even when we regard ourselves as hired hands.

"Hungry?" was the first word to follow the hug. We had flown our own plane into Pontiac Airport and the hour was early. Kate knows we like to eat light and fast when shooting video and she had already asked Steve about the prospects of nailing a fresh bagel or two. Steve knew just the place.

The line was out the door when we pulled up to The Bagel Place in shiny clean Keego Harbour. No problem, the service was as fast as it was friendly. And obviously, Steve was a regular as he was immediately greeted by name and handed the bagel of his choice even as he was staring into the full display case. They know Steve. They know bagels. And apparently, they know Steve's bagels!

The next day we were to meet Steve at the store. Kate offered a bagel stop and didn't need to beg for agreement.

Once into The Bagel Place, a smiling woman behind the counter remembered me from the day before and reached automatically for a cinnamon raisin bagel. She was living proof that women can be cute in their teens, pretty in their twenties, but not beautiful until thirty. She might have been French, but beauty translates pretty well without regard to nationality.

"Where's Steve?" she smiled.

"We left him at the store."

"Then be sure to take him his bagel. It's on the house!"

Back in the van I remarked that this kind of random surprise was the very heart of Positively Outrageous Service. Customers remember the little things, those little acts of thoughtfulness that create loyalty and a sense of welcome.

Back at the store we presented Steve with his unexpected prize and again remarked that the folks at The Bagel Place practiced POS even if they didn't have a name for it.

"Oh, that's nothing," Steve hinted that he was about to top our story, and he did.

"Not long ago one of our managers stopped for a bagel on his way to work. When he reached for his wallet, he realized that he had left the house without either wallet or cash. The owner just handed over the bagel and said that he could take care of the bill the next time."

"Nice story," I said, having heard a dozen variations on the theme.

"But that's not all! When he handed over the bagel, there was a twenty-dollar bill in his hand. Our manager didn't get it at first, so the owner said, 'Take the twenty, too! I can't let you go all day without any money in your pocket.'"

And that's my latest favorite story of Positively Outrageous Service. Random and unexpected, out of proportion to the circumstance, involves the customer in an intimate way, and of course, creates compelling, positive word-of-mouth.

If you had been on the receiving end of POS like that at The Bagel Place, would you tell anyone about it? You bet you would! Would you become a loyal customer if you weren't already? Again, you bet you would!

And that is the power of Positively Outrageous Service. It's the Law of Harvest taken to work. What goes around really does come around. And the surprising part is that it comes around so fast. Great bagels, personal, Positively Outrageous Service—no wonder the line stretches out the door!

Whatever your business, Positively Outrageous Service can work for you. We work with nearly one hundred organizations every year, and so far, we haven't found a single one where Positively Outrageous Service didn't apply.

And, it's infectious—even in relationships!

We are fortunate to have Vickie to house-sit our dog, Bailey, when we travel. Vickie understands fun—and Bailey. Now, Bailey is not an ordinary German Shepherd. No, she has style. Ever since her first shower, she has accepted wearing a bandanna and knows when she is "naked." Here is Vickie's note to us following a short stay:

> *Scott and Melanie,*
>   *Bailey told me she really didn't like this outfit. I thought she was kidding with me until I came home Thursday. She had ripped her clothes from her body and proceeded to rip them to shreds—twelve pieces to be exact.*
>   *I guess Bailey was serious, she really didn't like it. I asked her why and she told me it made her look fat. (I didn't know where you keep her "outfits" or I would have dressed her.)*
>   *—Vickie*

POS HAS NO LIMITS!

Shelley Kusch is the General Manager of Kuleto's Trattoria in Burlingame, California. Kusch is a food pro; but, more important, she and her crew are experts at delivering Positively Outrageous Service.

When the administrative assistant of a regular client called to reserve space for a large party, Shelley and staff knew instinctively that the evening was intended to be very special (a suspicion that was confirmed when the client and guests arrived).

The administrative assistant made several more calls to review the menu and wine selections and was pleased that two top servers, Carolyn and Tony, had been assigned to the party.

When the host arrived with his guests, it was quickly apparent that the wine selections, while excellent, weren't quite as special as he had in mind. Garrett Harker, the assistant general manager who also serves as wine buyer, was quickly alerted and, in a matter of minutes, brought from the cellar several reserve selections that are highly valued for their rarity and fine quality. The guest was delighted.

Now the challenge was to see how to make every aspect of the evening memorable.

Garrett suggested port for after dinner and, even though he carried a fine 1977, suggested that he could send out to a local wine shop for something with even more character. Garrett offered to personally oversee the wine service. Cognac and Grand Marnier 1827 were served.

The guest was also getting in the spirit, no pun intended, when he waved Garrett to the table and said, "One thing that would really make my night would be a cigar."

No problem. Garrett set out to find twenty fine cigars, a feat that would be relatively simple during regular business hours but somewhat more difficult at 7:55 in the evening.

One local store answered the phone and when asked about closing time said, "Eight." When asked if he could wait an extra five minutes, the reply was a simple, "Nope. We open at nine tomorrow. Come in then."

Garrett persisted until he found someone interested in

doing business and sent a runner to make the purchase, topping off an evening of flawless customer service.

As the customer said good-bye to his guests, he said that he had eaten in the finest restaurants the world over and that this night had been truly special.

CHARGED UP

Jack Moody sent me the story about a Bloomington, Indiana, man who sells batteries—and gives away Positively Outrageous Service. Our service hero is named Jim Riordan, owner of Bloomington Battery Specialists. Jim makes service calls, something you don't see too often these days.

"I remember a call I got at 2:00 A.M. from a car out on the interstate. When you go that far, you want to make sure you've got the right battery, so I took three with me. The guy was from Rockford, and he said he was so pleased, he'd send me another customer.

"I thought, sure, from Rockford. But, two weeks or so later, here comes this guy from Rockford for a battery!"

(What I like most about this guy is that he works on "customer time.") After regular business hours, "I transfer the calls to my home. If I answer, I'm open."

AFTER HOURS

When our kids were visiting one evening, our daughterette was admiring a large dresser made to accommodate a television in the guest bedroom.

"If you ever decide to get rid of that, I'd like to buy it. It would go perfectly in our bedroom."

"Sweetie, anything in this house is yours for the asking. If you see it and you like it, you can have it. Would you like to take it now?"

Now, our son was dying a thousand deaths. He knew

that I would give the sweetie (and him!) anything, no questions asked.

"Well, maybe when we move to the new house," said the Nikster.

"It's yours. Would you like the rest of the set?"

"Only if you are sure that you don't want it."

Last week, they moved to the new house and it made good sense to part with the set, except that we had company coming.

"Come and get the dresser. We'll only need the rest of the set for a few more days until our company leaves."

On Sunday, two days before our guest would arrive, Melanie and I decided that the set would look great in their new house and set out to dismantle the room. We planned to run out and buy a new bed, and maybe a night stand and chest for the guest bedroom.

"Yo, Kiddo!"

"Hi, Dad!"

"Mom and I are loading the bedroom set for you. We'll bring it right over."

"Gee, thanks! What are you going to do for your company?"

"We'll go over to Rick's Furniture and pick something."

"I'm sure they're closed. Wait! I'll call the owner at home."

This story is already long and you can guess what happened. One of the owners finished his golf game, met us at the store, and gave us a terrific discount (aided by our kiddo who managed to slip in a healthy contribution without saying) and delivered the new furniture the next day in time for our company.

Would you be willing to do that for a customer?

WHEN IT RAINS . . .

Our home sustained major flood damage on July 19th. Saturday evening around 8 P.M. our State Farm agent arrived at our home with a grocery bag full of pop, chips, pine cleaner, even a potted rose bush. I never dreamed of such kindness from an insurance agent, especially after learning that she was out checking on her clients rather than cleaning up her own flood-damaged home!

MEN'S WEARHOUSE AT THEIR FINEST IN DALLAS

"I was greeted by Mr. Thomas and immediately taken to a wide choice of fine suits. He selected six suits of differing materials, fabric, and style. I chose one, realizing that I needed alterations on the trousers greater than simple hemming. Mr. Thomas expertly marked the waist and seams that needed to be taken apart and resewn. A beautiful woman performed magic on my trousers while other employees helped me select a tie to match my new suit perfectly.

"Within thirty-five minutes, I had purchased a suit, had it tailored, purchased a tie, and met three very impressive Men's Wearhouse employees.

"I have lots of choices when picking a store to buy men's clothing; department stores are too high priced, too little service. Or there are wholesale places that offer wide selection and no service. Your stores offer a fine selection and great prices. But what really makes the difference is the service!"

LEMONADE?

Mom hit Norwest Bank in Kerrville one hot Friday afternoon. Well, she didn't really 'hit' the bank, but you get the drift.

Under a tree near the drive-through, a few bank employees, looking very "unbankerish" in Norwest T-shirts and shorts, had set up an old-fashioned lemonade stand. They served their surprised customers with this unexpected offering of lemonade and Positively Outrageous Service!

DOUBLEGOOD

In early June a large delegation from Montgomery, Alabama, was leaving Washington, D.C. They had traveled by bus to participate in the Stand Up for Children Day. En route home, their bus decided to pull up lame. The good news is that it happened in front of the DoubleTree Park Terrace Hotel.

"Our group was forced to wait long into the chilly night. Hot coffee (and, of course, the famous DoubleTree cookies) were put out for us. One woman, Mammae, was particularly considerate. When we thanked her for her kindness, she responded, 'I know what it's like to be stuck and trying to get home.' She also told us, 'It's not me doing this—it's Double-Tree!' "

DON'T CRY OVER THESE ONIONS!

A story from CompuServe extols the virtues of Pennington Catering of Santa Ana, California. It seems that Pennington had been retained to cater an employee party when one employee, allergic to onions, inquired of a server about the possibility of onions in the hors d'oeuvres. The server promised to check and returned within minutes with a specially prepared tray of goodies, made by the chef who had been working out of a vacant office on site.

The writer made a point of mentioning Pennington and that she would be certain to use them again!

COFFEE, ANYONE?

Glenn Brill of Fox Cities Convention & Visitors Bureau in Appelton, Wisconsin, writes of a meeting planner from his group who was staying at the Valley Inn in Neenah, Wisconsin. She got up early, before 6 A.M., to prepare for her meeting and, needing coffee to function properly, was disappointed to discover that the kitchen was not yet open.

No problem! A housekeeper wandered by and, being empowered by her employer to do whatever it takes to solve guest problems, opened up the kitchen and made fresh coffee!

Funny, it's the little things that make the biggest impression.

EGGSACTLY RIGHT!

Joanne Schlosser writes to praise the Arizona Biltmore. And why not? I've sampled their hospitality a time or two myself.

Joanne has an allergy to eggs. So what? Well, do you know how it feels to be served a dessert of fruit when the rest of the world is eating something special? Made aware of Joanne's special needs, the Biltmore folks created several egg-free desserts just for Joanne so that she could fully enjoy a special event at the property.

Think that only expensive hotels deliver POS? Well, think again! The Scottsdale Embassy Suites also answered Joanne's request for an eggless stay. They created a wonderful chocolate mousse made from whipped cream rather than egg whites.

And the hotels? They earned Joanne's loyalty for life!

On my last visit to the Biltmore, I took a short walk around the grounds. They are no less than stunning, a perfect compliment to this Frank Lloyd Wright–designed work of art. Passing a groundskeeper, I commented on the unusual brick that he was installing. He stood straight and asked if I was a fan of Wright.

"Who isn't? He was a genius."

With that, he spent nearly ten minutes explaining that the brick was from a mold designed by Wright and only used on this particular site.

Joanne got whipped cream. I got a brick story. We both got Positively Outrageous Service!

FAST POS

The DoubleTree Inn in Houston wanted to make check-in hassle free. They created a system where the PBX operator, upon receiving requests for airport pickup, would notify both the van driver and the front desk. This enabled the driver to welcome the guest by name and for the front desk person to pull portfolio, key, and cookies, resulting often in checking in the guest in thirty seconds or less!

SAFE AND SOUND

From Ann Devers of the National Air Transportation Association: "Scott: This is a company that lives POS!"

The company is ITS, the folks who provide airport security and skycap service.

Employee Emanuel Selassie saved a little boy's day, but just "bearly." The kiddo never travels without his stuffed teddy bear. Well, almost never. When the family arrived at the airport, teddy turned up missing.

Grandmother raced home, discovered the wayward bear hiding in a closet, and raced back to the airport where she tagged "runner" Selassie. Acting on little information and lots of energy, Selassie located the plane and delivered the bear just moments before takeoff!

Same company, this time a business story.

On July 26th, ITS started five accounts with less than two hours notice! Believe it or not, just after lunch a panic call came into the ITS offices. The company that held the contract for security in five cities from Anchorage to Salt Lake City was going under.

Could ITS save the day? Otherwise, thousands of travelers would be stranded.

Acting on faith and in record time, ITS sent paychecks to the employees who had not been paid by their former company, even negotiating equipment and office space leases.

How's that for Positively Outrageous Service—and smart business!

THE COFFEE THING

Bill Blum, now director of marketing for the beautiful Sonoma Mission Inn and Spa, used to work in "the pit," at least that's what they called the small area that housed the room service department at the Hyatt Regency San Francisco. When Bill worked there, things would "get crazy," and the crew would look for things to do that would relieve the tension.

One of their favorite things to do was to "figure out ways to blow the guest away" (with great, but surprising service).

"Our favorite had to be 'the coffee thing.' I call it that because all I had to say to our favorite busboy Ron (who I believe is still there) is, 'Do you want to do the coffee thing?' And he would start salivating like a retriever when you show him a tennis ball. Ron was always a mess from picking up trays, so we didn't allow him much guest contact. But he had exclusive rights to 'the coffee thing.'

"The coffee thing was simple. We received literally dozens of orders each morning simply for a pot of coffee for two, and would set the trays up specifically for those orders with everything ready to go, except the hot coffee. When I would tell Ron it was time, he would take one of the trays, fill the thermal pot with coffee, hold a room service elevator at our level, and we would wait.

"Sure enough, in a few minutes, a guest would call for a pot of coffee for two. And Ron's eyes would light up like we just caught a twenty-pound trout. In the middle of the order, I would ask the guest if they could hold for just a moment. While they were holding, I would quickly ring up the check, give it to Ron, and he would be off with the order. I would come back on the phone, apologize for putting them on hold, and then proceed to slowly and deliberately ask their name and room number (which we didn't actually need because it appeared on the screen when they called). Then I would repeat the order, repeat their name and room number, and total the bill for them.

"Before I finished, there was usually a knock on the door. I would say, 'Is that someone at the door?' They would usually reply, saying, 'Yes, I'm sorry . . .' I would interrupt them and say, 'Actually, it's no problem. That should be your coffee.'

"When Ron was unable to make it before I got off the phone, I would tell them, 'Let's see, please give us twenty to thirty seconds for that order.' Usually they would question the time and go 'seconds?' and I would go into this story about how we liked to serve our guests as quickly as possible, etc. Inevitably during the conversation, Ron would make it to the room and knock on the door.

"This game not only produced many of our best comment cards for our department, but it was great for morale, Ron's tips, and always it left the whole department grinning, particularly the sight of Ron coming off the elevator panting and saying, 'Okay, let's do it again.' "

A GOOD NEIGHBOR WRITES!

"One of my customers and his son were on their way to California when they rolled their vehicle in New Mexico, totaling it. The mother and son were sent to a hospital in Grants, New Mexico, while their car was towed to Thoreau.

"It was 5:45 P.M. when I was contacted. I had been at the office later than usual due to the heavy claim volume from a hailstorm the week before. He asked me what we could do. He had no car, no car rental, no way to get to California and he didn't know anyone in New Mexico.

"My first call was to the Springfield claims office. Again, due to the large claim volume from the hailstorm, I was able to catch someone at 6:00 P.M. They gave me the numbers to the nearest claim service office, Gallup, New Mexico.

"Just before ten o'clock, the phone rang again. It was my customer, calling to tell me that his wife and son were being moved to Albuquerque for further testing. I asked him to get the phone book and read me the names and home phone numbers of the first three State Farm agents.

"I called a perfect stranger and said, 'I'm a State Farm agent in Illinois, calling to ask you for some Outrageous Service. Would you be willing to go to the hospital and pick up my customers, take them to a motel and see that their claim gets handled quickly?'

"Her answer was, 'Which hospital?'

"Three hours later she called to say that they had been released and were safely checked into a motel. By the way, this hospital was an hour from her home and she offered to pay for the motel, and even loan the use of her credit card to pay for the rental car! Needless to say, my customers were thrilled!

"P.S. My customers are home now and have increased their coverage. They also say that they will never again ignore our suggestions about coverage or complain about price!"

And another good neighbor . . .

"My agent and employer has a client insured under a State Farm tenant's policy who is mentally handicapped. One day the client called, very upset because someone had stolen his adult tricycle. (Because of his handicap, this was his only transportation.)

"Not being successful locally, my boss went to the cycle shop in the next town and found a replacement. The tricycle was too large to fit into his station wagon so he borrowed a truck to pick up our customer. Together they went to pick up the new tricycle. And, my boss then personally purchased a lock for the new tricycle.

"We aren't kidding when we say, 'Like a good neighbor, State Farm is there!'"

A ROSE IS A . . .

Have you ever been to Butchart Gardens in Victoria, British Columbia? If you haven't, go! It's beautiful.

And it's even prettier if you are eighty!

The gardens has a special promo for persons turning eighty years old. Maxine Glover will finish the tale:

"My father recently took my mother and I there for his special day. Here is what happened: As we drove up to the ticket window, my father showed proof of age. The ticket seller put a special ticket on the window and directed us to the VIP parking lot, right at the entrance. After enjoying the gardens, we were to experience 'tea' at Butchart Gardens.

"The complimentary tea included our choice of any non-alcoholic beverage. We were instructed to sit where we liked in the dining room and our tea would be brought to us. We each received a lovely plate of finger sandwiches, a warm scone with small pots of butter and strawberry jam, a cookie, a fancy pastry and a strawberry dipped in chocolate.

"While we were enjoying our tea, a server came to take Polaroid pictures ('One for us, and one for you to take home!')"

Would service like that cause you to tell the world? Well, it worked for Maxine and Butchart Gardens!

HOLD THE MAYO

"It was just after midnight," wrote a very pleased DoubleTree guest, "and because of my schedule I was unable to have dinner. I went to the bar near the check-in area in search of something, anything, to eat.

"I know now that you folks actually mean it when you say, 'We'll do everything we can to satisfy your needs,' because Paul the bartender went into the kitchen and prepared a great turkey sandwich with all the trimmings and a pasta salad."

Not bad from a kitchen that was closed!

THANKS FOR THE MEMORIES

There is nothing sweeter to a customer than being remembered. And you don't have to remember a name to do the job, just remember.

A Denny's customer wrote: "You remembered after almost six months that I like my tea with cream and extra spoon, because I like my eggs poached soft and don't like egg yolk in my tea."

Okay. So maybe that customer is a little . . . unusual. But remembering builds loyalty, even among the terminally picky!

DR. DENNY'S

Do you think special requests are reserved for the high-priced joints? Well, think again!

A business that coordinates arrangements for cancer patients puts them up at a California hotel because there is a Denny's next door. When the manager heard that cancer patients sometimes require special meals, his only response was, "No problem!" He immediately set out to add special meals for his special guests.

Not only is this good for the body, it's good for the soul. And, as a side benefit, it's good business, too!

JUST GET ME TO THE CHURCH!

Two State Farm policyholders were having "one of those days." Their son was getting married, and they were on the way to the airport to pick up two of the bridesmaids to attend a shower.

Already running late, the situation worsened when the car would not restart at the airport. The husband then recalled State Farm's theme: "Like a good neighbor, State Farm is there." So he looked in the Yellow Pages and called State Farm for help.

The agent who answered the phone dropped everything, pushed back a few appointments, called a tow truck, and headed for the airport thirty minutes away. A mechanic was located but could not fix the car in time for them to make the wedding shower sixty miles away.

The agent drove them! Now that's buy-in on a slogan!

PUTT-PUTT COOKIES

When he was manager of the DoubleTree at Houston Intercontinental, Bob Van Bergen set out to add a little POS to the often harried nature of an airport hotel.

His director of guest services, Pat Savage, decided to lighten the wait of the usual rush from 5:00 to 7:00 P.M. at check-in by setting up a small putting course in the lobby. Guests waiting to check in were invited to putt for a tin of cookies. Bob says that even nongolfers participated, and some wanted to try over and over until they won!

ABSOLUTELY, POSITIVELY

You have to get up pretty early to "out-POS" the master, but that's exactly what the good people of Federal Express Customer Service did when I keynoted to their annual customer service seminar in Williamsburg, Virginia.

Each attendee had received a copy of POS several weeks before the event and took to heart the suggestion that they read the book before arriving in Virginia. (Boy, does that make a difference in the audience's understanding of the concept!)

Peggy Gaston of Federal Express corporate had what I think is the most fun, touching, personal idea ever. A copy of POS was put on the registration table and each attendee was invited to autograph the book. Now there's a twist! Usually I am the one doing the signing!

I was presented with this wonderful gift of nearly four

hundred signatures, with many listing their home locations from around the world. Many of the signers chose a page or chapter that was especially important to them and quite a few made comments explaining why.

Random, unexpected, out of proportion to the circumstance, and definitely, it's the story that I can't wait to tell!

For more T. Scott Gross . . . www.tscottgross.com

SIXTEEN

POS Marketing

Would you like to turn up the volume on your marketing? How about a neat idea or two for leveraging the marketing that you are already doing? Well, it's not all that complicated. It takes a little creativity and a healthy appetite for risk. If you can stand the heat, you'll love cookin' up a good dose of Positively Outrageous Marketing.

There are four characteristics of POS Marketing, but, as you might guess, like its cousin Positively Outrageous Service, surprise is a key ingredient.

One test of Positively Outrageous Service is that if you cannot tell where service stops and marketing begins—that's probably POS. POS creates positive, compelling word-of-mouth through surprising, out-of-proportion customer service. Apply the same rule to marketing and what do you get? Marketing that is talked about. If you can get customers to talk about your marketing, son, you've done gone and done something powerful!

Here's the test for POS Marketing: Is it newsworthy? Answer "yes" and you're on the right track.

FOUR POINTS OF POS MARKETING

Point One: Fun!

We found that if you can create programs that are fun, involve the product, get people to the property, and (this is a big one) do something good for others, you'll have a knock-down marketing event.

Fun is a key element of Positively Outrageous Marketing. We aren't the only ones who have discovered that the element of fun amplifies any marketing effort.

From the file, I bring you an ad for Dick's Last Resort in San Antonio. Before we go further, take notice of the company name, Dick's Last Resort. It tells you right up front that this is going to be a good time. In fact, the name is also a warning. It lets you know from the get go that if you are feeling grumpy, keep your grouchy backside outside!

The ad that caught my attention is headlined "Elvis Lives." It dares the reader to "come see for yourself" as they celebrate his sixty-first birthday and notes that if you enter the Elvis karaoke contest and dress the part, you earn "suck-up points."

We're talking pure, unadulterated f-u-n. Nothing exotic. Nothing fancy. Just goofin' off.

And guess what? People like that. In a world that is far too serious, a little fun draws a lot of attention.

Is any idea too corny? Not if your name is Insurance Man aka Dennis Savage of Springfield, Oregon. I'm holding one of Dennis's cards, which proclaims that his policyholders are "protected by Insurance Man." And yes, there is an Insurance Man costume: leotard, cape, and I hate to say what else! In an area with nearly fifty competing agents, standing out is the secret to survival, and a caped insurance crusader tends to stand out!

At Borders Bookstore in Austin, we spotted an outline of a body neatly chalked on the floor in front of a sales section featuring, you guessed it, murder mysteries.

Next to fun, there is nothing like a good story to grab your customer. I guarantee you that if you share any part of this book with a friend or co-worker, it will be a story. No matter how hard I try to be serious, when I go out to speak, people who have heard me make a point of saying, "Be sure to tell the Bubba story." Why? Because when you hear a good story, you become a part of the action. You put yourself in the place of the hero, or maybe you just share the word picture so clearly that the story becomes real.

The Wall Street Journal reported a hugely successful ad campaign by HIP, Health Insurance Plan of Greater New York, that used humorous stories to capture the viewer. Such things as a construction worker getting whacked by a board, a woman leaping over a tennis net to congratulate her opponent only to trip and tumble, and a passerby who is about to get clobbered by a falling piano were used to tickle funny bones while watching commercials about broken bones. Why the interest? Humor and stories.

(Melanie, my wife and editor, could not sway me to modify the term "humorous," which I used to describe these rather oddball commercials. And I want to go on record, she threatened to whack me to see if it was humorous!)

Is there a better example than the serialized commercials for Taster's Choice? You remember the two middle-age, single neighbors who turn borrowing instant coffee into a relationship that seemed to last forever. Well, consumers apparently were glued to their sets waiting for each new commercial for the next turn in the relationship.

My newest favorite? The "Got Milk?" campaign that features a deceased attorney who winds up in a world filled with chocolate. After he stuffs himself with chocolate everything, he heads to a fridge stuffed with milk cartons, all of which are empty. With a chocolate-lined mouth, he panics and says, "What kind of place is this?"

The commercial ends simply with, "Got Milk?"

Point Two: Involve the Product

In Bunol, Spain, we find the ultimate example in the annual La Tomatina, which is probably the world's largest food fight. Do they attract a crowd? Over a half million line the streets as huge trucks haul millions of tomatoes to the waiting crowds.

The vegetable equivalent of the running of the bulls held in Pamplona, La Tomatina puts fun (and what soon amounts to tomato puree) into the streets. Some wear goggles and helmets, but most of the crowd wears old T-shirts and cutoff jeans as they pummel friend and stranger alike with soft red tomatoes. How's that for involving the product?

Shopkeepers hose down participants, which lessens the sting of citric acid from the tomatoes. After the event, fire hoses wash the tomatoes into the storm sewers while participants head to public showers. (The citric acid acts as a cleaning agent so the event leaves the streets and buildings sparkling.)

Tea Time

A nice lady from the March of Dimes asked if we would help sponsor the big annual event. What she had in mind was a couple of hundred bucks to help provide T-shirts for the participants. Of course, we would get our logo printed on the shirts. And, of course, I said, "No."

She was shocked. "You sponsor everything," implying that she couldn't imagine me turning away such a worthy cause as March of Dimes.

"Yes, ma'am, but not this. You want me to spend a couple of hundred bucks to encourage people to walk on the other side of town. Now, I'd be delighted to play, but this isn't it.

"If you're willing to start and end the march at my store, I'll play in a big way. First, I will give everyone who starts the march a hot honey-butter biscuit." (It's my theory that all good marketing is aimed at getting trial. If you have a great product and people try it, you've probably won a customer. So I like to focus all my marketing on encouraging trial.)

"Not only that, but when the folks return, I'll give them a cold cup of tea."

Here, we were playing to my cheap side. There is absolutely nothing in tea! It is the cheapest thing a restaurateur can serve. Heck, if you have high iron content in your water, you don't even have to put the tea in the tea!

"Annnd," I said, upping the ante another notch, "I'll have the Chicken Man lead the march!"

"You can do that?" she exclaimed.

"Lady, I know him personally!"

Now I should probably describe this suit even though there is not a big point to be made.

It featured green knee socks, yellow baggy shorts, an orange top, and white, custom, fur wings. Are you getting a picture here? There was a rubber beak, wraparound mirrored sunglasses, and a white hard hat on which we had stuffed and mounted a real chicken! As chicken suits go, this one was truly awesome!

(In fact, when we sold the store a couple of years ago, we kept the suit. Melanie likes me to wear it around the house every now and then!)

The question is this: "If you were the photographer for the local paper, what picture would you take? Several hundred people in look-alike T-shirts or a guy with a chicken on his head?"

I rest my case!

Now the march takes about two hours. We started it about nine-thirty. What time do these tired, hungry folks get back to my store? (Hint: Eleven-thirty is not the right answer!)

Point Three: Get 'em to Your Property

If the goal of marketing is to get trial, then it follows that you want to hold as many marketing events as possible on your turf. At the very least, make folks come to your place to register or pick up prizes. Best of all is to get them to your property, no matter what.

Ever been to Lund, Nevada? No? Well, neither have many others. For you and me, that's not a problem. But if you are trying to run a business in that tiny town, you might be looking for a way to attract a crowd. And why not with the Silver State Classic Challenge, a road race open to the general public run on a state highway?

Average people race average cars in this "anything-but-average" race, where in the open class so-called average speeds can average 186.73 mph (faster than the 147.956 record average for the Indy 500).

You could sign up if you wanted. Anything that rolls is pretty much okay. How about a 1989 Ford Taurus or a 1965 Olds Cutlass? These are but two of recent entrants.

The point? If you are going to produce a POS Marketing event, for goodness sake, get 'em to your property, involve your product, and have a good time! If there is a formula for attracting attention, this is the recipe! Of course, if you really want to hit a home run, add one final ingredient: Do something good for others.

Point Four: Doing Good for Everyone!

Personally, I can't imagine a POS Marketing event that didn't involve this final element, doing something good for others. Why? Because I'm a good guy? I'd like to think that has something to do with it. Let's assume the worst, that I am a mean, selfish, capitalist pig. Then what would I do? Same thing!

When your promotions involve doing good for others, magical things happen. Suddenly you have a partner who has a vested interest in the success of your promotion. To add frosting to the cake, you are perceived as being a community supporter.

I can't tell you how many times we've had people tell us that they were glad we offered good product. Why?

"Because of the good things you do in the community, we'd have to eat here even if it wasn't that good!"

IMAGINATION

The one thing you need for Positively Outrageous Marketing is imagination. That and the willingness to take a risk, to perhaps "crash-and-burn" from time to time.

To create an idea for Positively Outrageous Marketing, practice this: Take two or more ordinary ideas and smoosh them together.

We received a card from Sergio Tardio announcing that the former chef concierge of the Ritz Carlton, St. Louis, had moved his whisk to the Beverly Hills Hotel and Bungalows. Simple, inexpensive, creative. Not really POS Marketing, but unusual, so I mention it here. Hey! When was the last time you received an announcement like that?

Marx Gibson, general manager of *The Herald-News* in Joliet, Illinois, was reading *Positively Outrageous Service* while flying home on Southwest Airlines. The napping woman who was sitting beside him awoke and noticed what he was reading. It turned out she was a SWA employee and quickly pointed out that POS was "their service secret."

"If it's good enough for SWA, it might work for a newspaper" went Gibson's line of reasoning, so he started dog-earing pages and soon had cooked up a POS idea or two of his own.

The headline read:

Herald-News Boss: This Guy Delivers . . . On Your Street.

Look for Marx Gibson, delivering your paper, listening to your comments and complaints.

The lead sentence read "Tell it to da boss."

Gibson started riding with route carriers, helping them deliver papers, and knocking on doors.

"During our publicized walks through the neighborhoods, people gave us bags of fresh corn, invited us in for iced tea, handed several days worth of marked up newspapers to me, took our photos, and generally told us how much they appreciated the fact that the boss came to their door."

Simple, elegant, inexpensive, and dead-on POS!

COPYCAT AND PROUD OF IT!

Big Dave Ostrander of (naturally) Big Dave's Pizza & Subs in Oscoda, Michigan, took a page right out of the original *Positively Outrageous Service*. Dave surprises customers with the following letter that is attached to orders—whenever Dave feels like it!

> *Dear Friends:*
>
> *Old friends are essential in any business. Everyone at Big Dave's is committed to treating our guests like family. We feel that is one of the reasons we've carried on for the past twenty years. It's awkward to charge guests for a good time so . . . today is your lucky day. This entire order is FREE! In order to make this day possible, all of our staff is voluntarily working for free. Please treat them generously. Please feel free to tell your friends. Thanks for the opportunity to serve you.*
>
> *—Big Dave Ostrander and Crew*

CREATIVITY AT WORK

Here's one I read about. Now you're reading about it!

Kaufman & Broad Home Corporation decided that when it comes to creativity their employees were tops. To take advantage of this natural trove of talent, they gave each employee, all 1,200 of them, a T-shirt with the company logo and challenged them to see how much publicity they could legally get.

How did they do? Well, workers jumped out of planes, stopped rush hour traffic by parading en masse across a freeway overpass and even dressed an elephant in an appropriately sized version of the shirt.

What do you think your employees would do if similarly challenged? Try it!

In the mail bag, we found a Mercedes emblem with an offer to see the rest of the vehicle. What followed was a unique invitation to preview a new all-activity vehicle by Mercedes. This is the kind of marketing that, while expensive, certainly gets your attention. (While it's true that I drive a plain-Jane Ford pickup and an Explorer with a grill guard, I did keep the Mercedes emblem. You just never know!)

We were invited to present Positively Outrageous Service to the good folks in Baton Rouge. To grab the attention of local executives, they sent two clever versions of the invitation. One was an empty brown lunch bag imprinted with this simple message: "Who Says There's No Such Thing as a Free Lunch?" The other mailing included a wallet that contained tickets to the event and a card that promised so many money-making ideas that they would be needing another wallet. Pretty clever! Pretty POS!

～◦◇◦～

Here's a perfect example of POS Marketing. When the World Cup of Soccer tournament came to Washington, D.C., the folks at Galileo Restaurant prepared theme meals to honor the contestants: Italian menu one day, Norwegian the next and followed that with Bolivian food. They donated 20 percent ($900) of sales to the American Diabetes Association and were swamped with publicity.

Imagine what such exposure would cost if you could buy it. At $900 the event was a bargain, plus it did something good for others. Beat that!

SIGNATURE AND SOUTHWEST TAKE THE CAKE

Would you look at this? A POS "WOW" story that involves two of my favorite players!

Signature also handles fueling and baggage handling for commercial flights at a number of major airports. In Seattle, one of their clients is SWA. Here's the story.

"With the help of a few photographs, a local baker of exotic cakes was contracted by the folks at Signature to help create an edible miniature of an SWA B-737 with an edible Signature Flight Support fuel truck positioned to fuel the aircraft. The cake was done in the appropriate corporate colors down to the graphic elements of the Signature logo and a message that read, 'Happy First Anniversary Signature and Southwest.'

"The cake was in celebration of the first anniversary of the contract between the two service masters.

"The Southwest station manager had no idea what to expect when the entire Signature staff stepped into Southwest's operations area with this cake. The Southwest station manager was so impressed with the realistic aircraft and fuel truck that she didn't want to eat it, rather, she wanted it shellacked!"

What could you do that would qualify as Positively Outrageous Marketing? Could you put two disparate ideas in a head-on collision and create something special? Could you take a run-of-the-mill idea that "everyone" in the industry does and put a new twist on it?

Of course, you can! It just takes guts, imagination, and a touch of positively outrageousness!

SEVENTEEN

WOWs and Bloopers

Y ou're looking at the First Annual Service WOWs and Bloopers Award winners, or losers—if you think that way!

We've always told great stories about customer service but this year we're breaking a tradition and telling the worst customer service stories as well. There is one important distinction between our two lists. We've always figured that people already know how to give bad service, not much point in telling stories of awful customer service. Unless you can learn from those stories, which is what we will do with the Service Bloopers.

Another important distinction between our WOWs and Bloopers is that there are no names given to the "winners" of the Blooper Awards. Now if they wish to step up and claim the prize, well, that's their problem! We elected not to name the Blooper recipients for one important reason: It serves no useful purpose.

We have been franchisees of a major fast-food chain, and we suffered personally every time another store in the chain delivered poor service. You won't believe how many times we had customers tell us, "We don't normally stop at restaurants in your chain. We only stopped today because a friend told us

that your place is much better than the one near our home."
One bad apple really can ruin things for the rest of the group.

Every store is a mom-and-pop operation. No matter
whether the store is a little, locally owned independent or one
of a chain of superstores, somebody's ma and somebody's pa
are in charge. And we're not about to tar and feather a business based on what could well be an isolated incident.

In some respects, consumers who have a bad service experience have an obligation to complain, at least once. It is quite
possible that the store you are about to abandon is owned by
a hard-working couple who have their entire life wrapped up
in a storefront with a modest inventory of goods. These folks
may be struggling to provide you value in a world dominated
by retailing giants.

If you get unlucky and get poor service, tell 'em. Chances
are that they are unaware that you are dissatisfied. On the
other hand, if the owner personally gives you world-class
crappy service, tell me. We might be in the process of discover-
ing one of our next year's winners of the Service WOWs and
Bloopers Award!

WOW! **Air Traffic Control: Awarded for Consistent, Uncompromising Profession-
alism.**

Comment: The Air Traffic Control System falls under the
Federal Aviation Administration. In spite of the FAA's coming
under withering fire for its role in recent air traffic fiascoes,
the folks in Air Traffic Control (ATC) and their counterparts
in Flight Service Stations (FSS) across the country provide
absolutely, hands down, the best customer service anywhere
on the planet.

The men and women who guide the nation's aircraft
through intense traffic and weather of all kinds never seem to
lose their cool. Nor do they ever refuse to help a pilot who

may appear as nothing more than a blip on a screen, whose existence is little more than a scratchy voice on the radio.

The folks of ATC and FSS have been abused by a gutless Congress that has refused to allocate monies collected through use taxes reserved for improvement of the Air Traffic Control System. Instead, our congressional representatives hold this money hostage, fearing that if they allow it to be spent as designed the national debt will look as bad as it really is.

Every day, millions of Americans take to the air in long aluminum tubes, defying gravity, taking their chances that the 1960s technology that ATC employees must work with will hold up for another day.

If you ever have the opportunity to listen to the radio communications in a busy traffic control area, you will be amazed at how competent controllers can be under a veritable barrage of radio communications. Pilot after pilot checking onto the frequency, needing guidance and weather information. These heroes of the air, sitting in their darkened rooms, confidently and competently juggle several million pounds of metal and several thousands of lives traveling at hundreds of miles per hour. And they do it with style and humanity.

A salute to the men and women of Air Traffic Control and Flight Service Stations of the Federal Aviation Administration!

Story:

Every day there are hundreds of new stories of incredible service by ATC and FSS. This is just one, an example that only hints at the everyday heroism and humanity that are the gifts of nameless voices on the radio. This is just one of many.

WX Over Lubbock

The headwind was right on our nose knocking about twenty knots off the airspeed, making home seem just that much further. Since takeoff from Santa Fe, we had been sandwiched between layers of gray-blue clouds. One layer, kind of think and anemic, puffed harmlessly at about six thousand feet. We were at eleven, droning along and brushing the bottom of a rolling canopy that sometimes lowered to twelve but mostly held a little higher.

Close to Lubbock the view of center-pivot–irrigated fields became more and more occluded as the clouds on the lower deck began to huddle. It was as if they knew about the weather to come.

I knew about a hole, not in the cloud deck but in radio reception. A few miles to the southeast of Lubbock it is not unusual for controllers to call out your sign and warn that radar contact is lost. They pass you to the next center saying something like, "Mooney five mike kilo, contact Fort Worth Center on one three two point seven. If unable to contact, try again in one zero minutes. If still unable, try again."

Looking up, the horizon had gone nearly purple, a solid-looking mountain of cumulo-nimbus clouds in a sea of stratus nearly as gray as the thunderstorms floating in their midst.

"Center, Mooeny niner five mike kilo with a request."

"Five mike kilo, go ahead."

"Center, request permission to leave the frequency for a weather briefing."

"Five mike kilo, check back to this frequency as soon as possible."

Melanie dialed in Flight Watch and within seconds a deep, rich, clear-as-crystal voice was patiently delivering a command performance weather briefing into my headset. What service! On demand and just for me, a weather briefer is there to draw a mental picture of unfolding weather—here a front, there a lowering ceiling, winds at six, nine, twelve thousand or higher. The autopilot held the plane as I scribbled on the kneeboard and puzzled if I would need to make another plan.

Back with Center and firmly under the spell of the twenty-four satellites, feeding position data into my GPS, we had little to do but listen to radio chatter and watch the mountain of gray grow taller and darker.

On the panel the normally empty screen of the storm-scope began to sparkle. First one, then two, then a few bright green crosses pointing out the position of electrical activity. Airplanes can fly in rain and lots of it. What knocks planes from the sky is wind. Downdrafts that can push a plane to the ground at six thousand feet per minute while the plane makes a best-effort climb at a thousand feet per minute. (In round numbers that means your little plane will be a mile lower in the next sixty seconds. If the ground is less than a mile below, well, you get the picture and it just isn't pretty.)

The stormscope was mesmerizing. Little green gremlins would light their spot, capture your attention, and then disappear into the ether before you could look again.

"Mooney five mike kilo."

"Five mike kilo."

"Five mike kilo, flight service requested a call to advise you of weather in the San Angelo area that is causing some flight deviation. They said that this was not mentioned in your briefing."

"Center. Copy that. And thanks for watching out for us."

Did you get that? Somewhere in a darkened room, probably two hundred miles and a light-year away, someone was thinking about our little airplane. Someone who could go on break, drop a few quarters in a vending machine and pull the wrapper off a stale snack from the safety of a break room while we ran head-on into a wall of water and hail, downdrafts, and lightning powerful enough to rip the ailerons from the wings.

But he didn't.

Instead he called Center to say, "Have you got Mooney five mike kilo? You do? How about letting him know that since his briefing, we're seeing weather in the San Angelo area that might be reason to deviate from his course? Thanks."

And that was that. One more unseen service that made a difference to some unseen someone. Isn't that what makes life sweet? And don't tell me that those little acts of kindness don't register somewhere they can be counted!

WOW! Denny's Restaurants: Awarded for World-Class Social Responsibility.

Comment: You know the story. Several years ago Denny's was clobbered with a class action lawsuit charging them with racial discrimination. In short order, claims were coming out of the woodwork and attorneys were collecting megabucks.

Were they guilty? Probably so. But probably not nearly to the extent that the media frenzy may have indicated.

What impressed me (and should impress you) is how they handled the situation. Instead of hiding behind a veil of "no comment," the leadership took the heat and said, in effect, "We have a problem. We're not proud of it. We're going to fix it." And they did.

Last year I had the pleasure of presenting to their international franchisee convention, where the theme was "Remember When." It was a celebration of their thirteenth anniversary.

Some twenty years ago, I was a Denny's cook. It was a wonderful job. In fact, days after Melanie and I married (in spite of the fact that I was a junior executive for another company), I worked the breakfast shift at a local Denny's because I loved the work!

After the presentation Ron Petty, COO of Denny's, approached me to say that now that the civil rights action was pretty much handled, it is time to really work on the service piece. (As we speak, we are doing that!)

For now, I'd like you to meet a real service hero from Denny's, my favorite place!

Story:

I sifted through dozens of letters and hundreds of telephone call transcripts from customers who reported a wonderful Denny's experience. Many were as surprised as you that this much-maligned company would provide truly Positively Outrageous Service. Here is one of my favorites and, to tell you the truth, as nice as this story may be, it's hardly an exception.

A customer visited a Denny's competitor intending to take them up on the offer of a special birthday for his six-year-old son. He was shocked when his Birthday Club Celebration Card was refused; so, in a bit of a huff, he hustled off to a nearby Denny's Restaurant. There he complained to the Denny's staff about his rude treatment elsewhere.

As the family was finishing their meal, the entire staff surrounded the table, delivered a birthday cake complete with lighted candles, sang "Happy Birthday," and presented the child with a small stuffed animal.

The customer wrote to say, "Thank goodness for Denny's! They saved the day for one very happy little boy!"

And earned themselves a First Annual WOW Award!

WOW! **Signature Flight Support: Awarded for Setting the Standard in Customer Service.**

Comment: Late in August, we were flying into Meigs Field on the Chicago lakefront. A car was on reserve as was a tie-down space for our little Mooney. We were excited to be flying to a Signature Flight Support operation because we knew that they always deliver on their service promise.

Unfortunately, just as we were handed off to the approach controller, the ATC decided to close the field earlier than expected.

"Mooney five mike kilo, Meigs has just been closed due to an airshow. Say your intentions."

"Intentions? How about landing?"

"How about Midway?"

"Midway will do just fine, five mike kilo."

So there we were, heading to a runway buried deep in our chart book. We scrambled to locate the approach chart, airport diagram, and instrument landing system frequencies. All dialed in, we realized that our car was waiting at Meigs Field.

When we turned to our facilities guide, we were instantly relieved to discover that there was a Signature base at Midway. We knew that things would either be all right or they would make it all right.

On arrival at Signature, we were promptly marshaled to a parking space snug beneath the broad wing of a huge corporate aircraft that pretty much dominated the ramp.

Inside we were immediately greeted and invited to join them for lunch. Signature had just been voted the number one fixed base operator (FBO) in the industry, and to celebrate, they were throwing a party for their customers. We had Cajun chicken, barbecue ribs, potatoes au gratin, and a healthy portion of Signature service.

Story:

Signature Olé!

One of the best things about Positively Outrageous Service is that it is unexpected. Once you get in the habit of looking for opportunities to surprise, the possibilities seem endless. Masters of surprise and winners of one of this year's Service WOW awards are the fun folks at Signature Flight Services.

Since we fly our own plane, we get plenty of opportunity to sample the service at FBOs around the country. We've been pleasantly surprised by Signature a number of times.

The corporate aircraft of a well-known fast-food Mexican chain was due at the Signature base in Miami. Sensing an opportunity to WOW, one of the linemen ran to a local Mexican restaurant and borrowed a large sombrero and poncho.

Then he raced to the chain's closest local restaurant and purchased anything he could find that had the chain's logo on it.

Imagine the surprise when the Signature lineman, dressed in his Mexican garb, appeared on the ramp to marshal the aircraft to its parking space! The passengers and crew were escorted inside to a specially set table where they were treated to a feast of their own food.

The surprise was so complete that the guests could not be convinced that this had not been arranged by their own corporate staff!

WOW! **DoubleTree Hotels: Awarded for Service Leadership.**

Comment: DoubleTree Hotels have plenty in common with service leader Southwest Airlines. First, they have a CEO named Kelleher—no relation but a kindred spirit to the fabled Herb Kelleher of SWA. Second, they have Ann Rhoades, the goddess of personnel that Rick Kelleher brazenly stole from SWA.

We have seen and heard many organizations talk about creating a Positively Outrageous Service culture. At DoubleTree, they're doing it. If I had a pile of bucks to invest, I'd be buying DoubleTree stock. I recognize a winner when I see one!

Stories:

You get two stories because how likely is it that one chain could have two customer service stories that involve a shirt?

"Late on March 14th, our president arrived at the DoubleTree Hotel in Tampa.

"He went straight to his room and noticed on unpacking that he had everything he needed for his presentation the following morning—overhead slides, samples, handouts—even the Customer Appreciation Award. But he had forgotten one very important item, a clean dress shirt. At first he panicked, cursed a little, danced around his suite and even prayed.

"Desperate, he went down to the front desk where he met George, who had checked him in a few minutes earlier.

" 'George, I have a real big problem, and I need you to help me solve it!' George listened intently as our president explained that his presentation the next day was more than important, it was to be videotaped and used as a new product training tape at all of our customer locations nationwide. He asked George where, at such a late hour, a dress shirt could be purchased.

"George explained that a purchase was out of the question and asked our president what size he wore. When he replied, 'Size 16,' George smiled and said, 'You're in luck. I just picked up my laundry today and I wear size 16, too!'

"We have endeavored to make our company easy to do business with. We continually strive to employ associates who are customer-focused. How much easier and focused could you be than George who gave his shirt, if not off his back, out of his clean laundry to a desperate customer!"

And, story number two:

"As a pilot for Delta Airlines, it is my responsibility to ensure that the aircraft is in an airworthy condition prior to each flight. I'm required to perform a 'walk around' inspection of the aircraft exterior after every landing. This inspection requires me to walk under the aircraft, occasionally getting jet engine oil on my white uniform shirt.

"My crew checked into the DoubleTree in Tulsa late one evening. I asked the clerk that checked us in, Nicki, about the possibility of sending my oil-stained shirt to a local dry cleaners in the morning. Unfortunately, they would not be able to return it in time. Then I asked about the availability of washing machines but was again disappointed.

"With my options running out, it appeared that I would be stuck wearing an oil-stained shirt throughout the next day. Needless to say I was completely stunned when Nicki offered to take my shirt home, wash and iron it, and deliver it in the morning!

"In our busy, impersonal world it is not often that one comes across people who are so willing to help others in a time of need."

 Southwest Airlines: Awarded for Creating an Incomparable Service Culture.

Comment: The first time I visited Southwest Airlines's home office, in Dallas, I noticed a round, bald-headed man sitting between two flight attendants in the lobby.

"Who is that?" I asked.

I don't remember the exact answer but the gentleman had something to do with the flight attendant union. What surprised me was that this group didn't have the tightly set jaws that mark the usual "them versus us" looks that seem to be de rigueur for union folks.

My host noticed my surprise and said, "We have a great relationship with our unions. We think of them as part of the family. 'Love on' your people. That's what they want, that's what we do."

There isn't a group on this planet that I am prouder to be associated with, even if it's in such a tiny way. I like to think that maybe I'm a distant cousin in the SWA family.

Not long ago I kissed the El Paso runway in our little Mooney. As we taxied to the ramp, the ground controller cleared us ahead of a SWA 737 that was painted in the flag of Texas motif, which is very similar to the silver star, white and blue scheme on our Mooney.

There we sat, nose to nose, 737 and baby. I said to the tower, "Mooney five mike kilo will yield to our other company plane!" (The SWA ad slogan is "Take the company plane.")

I saw a 737 smile!

Story:

A favorite SWA story is supposed to go here, but they are all favorites. I suppose my "most favorite" SWA story is the one titled, "Christmas Man," near the front of this book. Naaaa! That's only my most favorite because it's new.

Okay. Here's my most favorite SWA story. It's also the secret behind their success, and this is so secret that even they don't know it. So, you're the first!

(The secret to SWA's success lies not in the stories that they tell but in the telling itself. Positively Outrageous Service, SWA style, is a matter of culture. And culture is a matter of stories. What makes SWA unique is their absolute dedication to "good-finding." They make heroes out of ordinary people by telling and retelling their stories. Tell the story. Build the legend. A service culture is born.)

Angel Wings

A Southwest Airlines customer wrote a letter telling that her fiancé had been killed in an airplane crash and continued by saying:

"On January 8, I flew from Houston to Phoenix for the funeral. My fiancé's dream was to someday receive his Captain's bars so that he could wear his uniform. As I deplaned, I asked the captain of our flight where I could find a set, and he took them off of his uniform and gave them to me to place in the coffin!

"I want to thank him for giving me a small sense of peace, showing that people care and proving that the world is not a terrible place."

Now you know why Southwest Airlines will probably win a Service WOW Award forever.

WOW! **Yankee Stadium Ground Crew: Awarded for Pure Showmanship.**

Comment: Showmanship was invented by peanut vendors. Movie theaters and circuses used to be the home of showmanship as were ball parks and county fairs. Somehow the art of showmanship was lost. Today the fun and entertainment is rarely seen in theaters other than what makes it to the screen.

A favorite San Antonio vendor sells anything and everything by simply yelling, "That's what I've got! That's what I've got!" It makes you look, doesn't it? If he yells "Peanuts! Hot Peanuts!", there is no need to turn your head if peanuts aren't your thing. By yelling "That's what I've got!", it grabs your attention. Grabbing and holding attention is what showmanship is all about.

My definition of showmanship is "giving a product personality—yours!"

When I first saw the Yankee Stadium ground crew drop the leads on the infield dirt drag and turn to do a dance routine to "YMCA" by the Village People, I nearly fell over. Here was an outstanding example of showmanship coming from probably the least likely group, the guys who cut the grass and smooth the dirt.

I thought, "If these guys have the chutzpah to perform 'YMCA' in baggy pants in front of a jaded crowd of thousands, there is no excuse for anyone not to be playful at work!"

The next time I saw these characters they were leading the world's longest "Macarena" line! Give me a break!

Story:

The Dragsters

You've seen 'em on *Dateline, Good Morning America!*, and in the World Series. Of course, they're The Dragsters, that wild and crazy grounds crew that drags the pitcher's mound at Yankee Stadium and, in the process, entertains the world with their version of "YMCA" or the "Macarena."

What started out in the minor leagues quickly moved to the majors when Debbie Tymon of the Yankee organization talked the grounds guys into trying their hand, er . . . feet, with "YMCA." Instant hit! And why not? What must be one of the most boring jobs in the world, dragging a mat across a pile of dirt, suddenly turns into pure showmanship with thousands of surprised and cheering fans.

When the "Macarena" craze hit, it hit the Yankees, too. Seattle was actually the first to attempt the "Macarena." The Mariners wanted to set a world's record. Debbie saw a PR opportunity. Let the Mariners have first hit and then beat them at their own game. She declared August 16th "Macarena" night.

Actress/dancer Chita Rivera came to rehearse the crew and perform with them in their first "Macarena" performance. On a night when the expected attendance was 30,000, over 50,000 turned out to cheer and dance their way into the record books.

On September 19th, with their now-expanded repertoire, the crew struck again, playing a double-header. "Macarena" game one. "YMCA" game two. These guys are versatile!

They're also an inspiration and prove that a little showmanship can make almost anyone in any job a star!

Says Rick Cerone of the Yankee organization, "There may be others, but they're not in the same league!"

WOW! **Kathie Lee Gifford: Awarded for Social Responsibility.**

Comment: After cereal and the *Today Show*, Regis and Kathie Lee take over our TV set. That's about the time we hit the off button and head for the office. One morning we were running a little late, still slipping banana slices to the dog when we caught Kathie Lee responding to charges that a line of clothing that she endorsed was manufactured by exploited sweatshop labor.

Kathie Lee nearly came unglued.

I think it was an honest mistake by an honest and caring performer.

Kathie Lee didn't let some PR goof attempt to sweep

things under the rug. Nope, Kathie Lee (with husband Frank Gifford) buckled up, went looking for the truth and did what she could to make things right. Now that's a service hero!

 National Tire Warehouse: Awarded for Consistent, High Service Standards.

Comment: If there is one outfit that I consistently hear good things about, it is NTW. We have, on a number of occasions, been blown away by their incredible dedication to service. In fact, NTW is one of the few automotive outlets where you leave feeling served not sold.

Shortly after deciding that NTW deserved to be listed here, we discovered that they had been bought by Sears, a company not known for service, to say the least. In search for service stories and details about the company, we called the NTW service hot line. No surprise here; we got a cheerful voice that immediately directed us to the NTW corporate number.

We weren't surprised when we called corporate. True to Sears' reputation, we got voice mail, an endless labyrinth of voice mail. (We've always said that voice mail was for companies that really wanted to offend their customers but didn't want to take the time to do so in person.)

After numerous attempts and no return calls, we finally reached a sunshine-voiced, real, live human being—in personnel! This got results.

So here they are, NTW, great customer servers now handicapped by their affiliation with Sears. Go figure. Actually, go buy tires before the Sears' corporate culture spoils the magic.

Story:

It's pretty typical for customers to pull into NTW right at closing and expect their tires to be replaced or repaired. And it's typical NTW to cheerfully do the work. So I won't tell you any one of the many stories of desperate travelers who have limped into NTW at closing to be saved by folks who care enough to put the customer ahead of artificial closing schedules. Instead, try this on for size:

A Virginia customer writes: "My wife and I had a flat and, because of the unusual tire size, it was difficult to locate a replacement (even from the dealer). I visited three other tire stores and each concluded that the tire could not be repaired and that a replacement would have to be ordered.

"But, at NTW, I was delighted to discover that you had the tire in stock. When I met your manager, he said that it was impossible to determine that the tire could not be repaired without first pulling it off the rim.

"Since the tire had only 5,000 miles on it, he recommended that we look carefully before deciding to replace it. In doing so, he determined that the tire could be repaired and thereby saved me $150!"

Another Virginia customer writes, "Last night, on our way home from work, my wife and I got a flat tire after running over a small, sharp piece of metal. I changed the tire and dropped my wife off at home before heading to your store. I arrived at 7:54 P.M. fully expecting that I would have to make an appointment or at least leave the car overnight.

"In addition to fixing my tire, the mechanic also replaced my spare and related hardware in my trunk exactly as they had been! At 8:16, a mere twenty-two minutes after arriving at your store, I drove out of the service bay!"

WOW! Men's Wearhouse: Awarded for Consistent, Excellent Service.

Comment: I first experienced Men's Wearhouse when a suit that I purchased at a major department store exploded. On my way to a television appearance, I stopped to call for directions. When I climbed into the rental car, the back end of my pants exploded, not ripped. Exploded!

The suit was only a year old and had not been worn more

than a few times. In the previous few years, I had purchased all of my suits at a certain department store. No problem, I thought. Problem. They gave me the third degree as if I had intentionally damaged the suit. I turned and left the suit, coat included, on the counter.

Across the street was a Men's Wearhouse. I had the idea that it was an el cheapo joint, but since I'm an el cheapo customer, I thought I'd give it a try. Boy, was I wrong! Low prices, maybe, but the service was first class. Within minutes I had a new suit picked out. Great price. Good quality. Just my style. What really blew me away was that the tailor was able to instantly hem the pants. No return trip, very convenient.

A few days later I received a postcard from the sales guy thanking me for my business. Wow! That's pretty classy! (The department store across the street had never sent me anything like that.)

A couple of months later the sales guy wrote to tell me about a sale on sports coats that would be perfect for the fall. I remembered mentioning that I would be needing a casual sports coat for the fall travel season. How did he remember?

I decided to check out the sale and, surprise! When I entered the store, my sales guy greeted me by name. I had only seen this guy a grand total of once, uno, a single time! Was I impressed!

You, too, will be impressed if you visit Men's Wearhouse. I like their commercials when founder George Zimmer closes, talking about the experience and says, "I guarantee it!"

For my bucks, Men's Wearhouse is the perfect combination of quality, price and service. And, oh, that service! This is the place where you are treated like a king! I guarantee it!

Story:
A satisfied customer with four kids and a mission descended on Men's Wearhouse.

"She began putting various items together creating three basic outfits. One, a suit, and two others consisting of a jacket and slacks. What amazed me was that the three could be mixed and matched to give me nine very different, very sharp combinations. And she did all this in a matter of thirty minutes. As we were finishing up, she explained that the fitting could be done instantly so that I could wear the suit for an important meeting the next day!

"We went to pay for the clothing and a young man appeared out of nowhere with my altered pants and pressed shirt, ready for the next morning. I was amazed.

"You have found another longtime shopper at Men's Wearhouse and I will be referring many to your stores. I GUARANTEE IT!"

WOW! Macaroni Grill: Awarded for Institutionalizing Showmanship and Quality.

Comment: I learned about Positively Outrageous Service from Phil Romano at Macaroni. The POS-heads who have been playing this game with me for the past few years know the story of Phil and his early days promoting the original Macaroni Grill, which is located in what was then the sticks outside San Antonio.

Being a single unit, Macaroni Grill was not what is known as "media efficient." In other words, there was no way with only one unit that Phil could expect traditional advertising to pay off since he would have to pay for advertising over a much larger area than he could expect from which to draw.

So Phil, in what has to be one of the most clever promotions of all time, decided to give away product. When you were young, you heard that the best kind of advertising is word-of-mouth. Phil set out to create positive, compelling word-of-mouth. He decided to do something so unexpected that customers would be forced to talk about Macaroni Grill.

Once a month, on a Monday or a Tuesday, and always completely unannounced, diners would receive not a guest check but a letter. The letter declared that their entire evening was on the house—drinks, entrée, dessert. The letter requested only that the waitstaff, which was working off the clock, be treated generously.

You can imagine how you would react if instead of having to shell out $40 to $60 for dinner and drinks for two, suddenly you were faced with a bill of zero, just leave a tip. Naturally, Phil's guests became instant Donald Trumps when it came to tipping. More important to the business, they became instant town criers, telling everyone and anyone about the Positively Outrageous Service they received at Macaroni.

Even today, four years after the last time Phil pulled that stunt, folks still are talking. A few arrive wondering if maybe this will be their lucky night.

Beyond being a promotional genius, Phil Romano is a showman. Phil understands that food is only part of the dining experience. In fact, experience is Phil's operating philosophy. He attempts to create and manage a total experience.

Does it work? Why not eat at a Macaroni Grill and find out for yourself why I have elected to award them with one of the First Annual Service WOW Awards!

Story:

Macaroni!

Do these guys understand service, or what!? I'll let a customer do the talking.

"On a recent visit to your Miami restaurant, I asked why the portobello-pesto mushroom soup was not offered more frequently. The general manager, Modesto Alcala, addressed my disappointment most courteously. He offered to have the soup prepared and delivered at my convenience. I declined his generous offer, but was most impressed with this young man's attention to a customer's request.

"A week later, Mr. Acala called to invite me to enjoy the mushroom soup prepared complimentary.

"Mr. Acala exemplifies excellence in customer service that

is not offered in most business establishments today. (I was pampered by the staff, as well!)"

And as the Lily Tomlin, character, would say, "and that's the truth!"

SERVICE BLOOPERS

There are millions or more stories about terrible service. Finding service bloopers is as easy as calling your neighbor. To qualify as a Service Blooper awardee, the story has to include an opportunity to set things right, an opportunity that was missed. We're not just looking for inattentive service or rude service. We're looking for world-class DUH service where the server had plenty of chances to set things right and, due to terminal unconsciousness, did not. These are the "best" of the worst.

☞ Bus (Don't) Stop: Awarded for Totally Misunderstanding the Job.

Comment: You cannot blame employees for doing stupid things when they are not trained and empowered to focus on a clear, customer-focused goal. In the story you are about to read, the employee involved was tightly focused on the wrong goal. Worse, so was his supervisor.

Story:

Of all the examples of poor service, this one surely takes the prize.

It was hotter than holy Ned, which is pretty hot. Closer than a wet sweatsuit, which is pretty close. I was as bored . . . oh, never mind.

I decided to kill an afternoon while waiting to speak. The guy draped over the bell stand promised me that the "big mall" was but a short bus ride away. So I decided to hit the road in search of frozen yogurt and a little exercise. "Blow the stink off," as Gran would say.

When I left the bus, I made a point of asking the driver about the schedule for the return ride. I don't recall now, but it seemed like he said, "Twenty past and ten till."

Yogurt was an easy find and by ten past I was waiting in the bright Florida sun. If you stand really still, you don't sweat. (And pigs can fly if they wiggle their tails.) By quarter past, I had concluded that, in some cases, operating on Lombardi time made no sense.

Twenty after, no bus. Half past, no bus. There are now at least twenty-five people standing in small pools of their own sweat, waiting for the bus which has by now been renamed the @#% bus!

Twenty till, quarter till, ten till . . . no bus. At five till . . . bus! Those who were standing leaned forward and waved pitifully. Those sitting climbed to their feet.

The bus didn't even slow down. It just drove right on by us!

About thirty yards away, the bus stopped. I ran. White shirt dripping into my dress shoes. The bus had stopped for crossing traffic so I raced. Bam, bam, bam! I hit the door. Squeeesh! It hissed open.

"Hey! You missed the stop! All those people are waiting on you. We've been there in the hot sun for nearly forty minutes!"

"Sorry." A small gush of air-conditioning swept out the open door. "I'm so far behind schedule that my supervisor told me to just run the route until I catch myself. He told me to get passengers on the next lap once I've caught up!"

The door hissed shut. The bus leapt into traffic. I took a cab.

☞ Two Bowls: Awarded for Being Completely Unconscious.

Comment: Do brain-dead clerks send you straight up a wall? Do you hate being ignored when you are a customer or potential customer? Well, don't blame the employee. Blame the boss for not hiring customer-centered employees and drilling them until there is no doubt as to what constitutes good customer service.

In this story the clerk had no idea that her job was to solve customer problems. She wasn't a bad person. In fact, I would bet that if she were to read this story, she wouldn't even recognize herself.

Story: *(See Chapter 8, pages 141–143.)*

☞ Pickup: Awarded for Completely Missing Multiple Opportunities to Recover.

Comment: This story is absolutely scary. It happened to us and was so awful that we couldn't believe that it was deliberate. In fact, we had an opportunity to go back a few weeks after it happened. And what do you know? The place was six kinds of wonderful!

The problem was that the situation was just far enough out of the ordinary that the manager was confused. I have a hundred dollars that given a chance to do it all over again, she would turn in a stellar performance.

Story:

Service stories seem to come looking for me. This great story found me one summer evening in Peoria.

I like stories for the lessons they teach. This story more than makes the point that when things go wrong, there is almost always more than a single solution. This is especially true for customer service issues. Read on, please.

Melanie and I had flown 95MK from Kerrville and we were hungry enough to eat a horse or any other properly prepared mammal. On the way in from the airport, the limo driver gave play-by-play commentary on the sights and attractions of Peoria. We listened only politely until he mentioned a restaurant that sounded especially good.

"The decor is as good as the food," he said. "They have

things imported from castles all over Europe. My wife and I come here when we want to have a really special evening. And, if you call them, they'll send their hotel limo to pick you up, so there's really no reason why you shouldn't give them a try."

Well, it turned out that there was a reason not to give them a try. In fact, we have several reasons. I'll tell the story; you make the call!

We called the retaurant and a delightful young woman promised that the limo would pick us up between 6:15 and 6:30. No problem. We were hungry. It was already 6:00. What would be another fifteen minutes or so?

At 6:10 we were waiting outside our hotel. We were still waiting at 6:30. And 6:35. And 6:40. I went inside to call.

"Sorry, Mr. Gross. We're not allowed to pick up non-hotel guests anymore. We called your hotel and tried to get the message to you."

(Time out. If this were your call, what would you have done when you discovered that you could no longer rely on your hotel to pick up non-hotel guests who were obviously standing outside their hotel waiting on a limo that would not come? Use your imagination. I can think of at least three ways to handle the situation and that's without thinking!)

I was furious. I called again, asking for the manager, and was connected with a woman named J.

"Ma'am. Let me tell you how we were just treated by your staff." I told her and minced no words in the process. "How would you feel if that had happened to you?" I wrapped up the very one-side conversation.

"Well, Mr. Gross, I guess I'd be pretty upset. But I want you to know that I called your hotel and asked them to tell you. They said that the bartender could find you and let you know. Maybe I should call and let them know they didn't follow through."

When it comes to service, some people never get it. Service is a no-brainer but you at least have to have one for backup!

If this were your call and you discovered that the guests had been left standing in spite of your attempt to contact them, what would you do?

Here are my thoughts—and don't read these until you have at least considered how this could have been handled:

Starting with the original promise that was quickly discovered to be unkeepable, you could have:

(A) Gone to the hotel bell stand, admitted that an error had been made, and asked for one last exception to the new policy.
(B) Sent a cab. (The trip was not more than a couple of miles and cabs routinely wait for fares right where your guests were supposed to be waiting.)
(C) Got into your personal automobile and retrieved the guests personally.

Okay, so maybe in the confusion of a dinner hour, you might have lost your head and failed to act at the first opportunity. But now, the guest calls. He is angry, but clearly he wants to be your customer or he wouldn't have bothered to call. Here are only a few of the things that could have been done:

(A) Apologize and tell the guest that you will arrange pickup within a matter of minutes.
(B) Apologize and tell the guest to jump into a cab and that you will pick up the tab for both the cab and dessert.
(C) Apologize and tell the guest that you will arrange immediate pickup and reserve the best seat in the house.

The really cool thing about customer service is that there doesn't seem to be any end to opportunities to make things right.

Let's say that you are a total numb-nuts and even after

the guest called to complain personally to you, the manager, you still didn't think to . . . think. The angry guest is now off the phone, it's past dinner, and you return to your senses. What do you do?

(A) Call the guest at his hotel, apologize and offer dinner for two the following evening.

(B) Call the guest's hotel, arrange for a plate of cookies or a late-night dessert to be delivered to their room along with a note of apology.

(C) Leave a handwritten note for the guest along with a gift certificate to be used at any time at your restaurant.

And what if you just read this and can't figure out what this is all about? GET AWAY FROM CUSTOMERS, including people who serve customers because you are the problem!

☞ Seven Minutes: Awarded for Allowing a Stupid System to Give Stupid Service.

Comment: Deming was fond of saying that the bulk of poor performance has more to do with the system than the performer. Certainly in this story, he has a point. Even though the system bears a lot of the responsibility, a little common sense would have made all the difference.

Story:
How can you fault someone for following policy? Easy. If they follow blindly and totally miss the point.

When we approached the airline gate, the agent told the two ladies immediately ahead of us to reclaim their baggage or risk a search. Now, these two suspicious middle-age women were not 10 feet from their bags. Obediently, they reclaimed their luggage and did the lift-shift-shuffle that makes waiting in line at airports such a pain.

When it was our turn, being experienced travelers, we

presented our tickets, and photo ID before being asked, saying, "We have received no gifts or packages from strangers. Heck, we didn't even get anything from people who know us! We packed the bags ourselves and they have been in our possession at all times. We each have a birthmark, but we can't let you see them!"

I've done that a hundred times and every time the gate agent has smiled, relieved that for once, they would not have to recite the litany of questions that have made traveling in modern times such an aggravation for everyone involved. Every time except this time.

Without skipping a beat, the gate agent said, "I need to ask you if you have accepted any gifts or packages from a stranger . . ."

"Ma'am?" I interrupted. "No gifts or packages from strangers, and the bags were packed by us and have been in our possession since."

"Sir," she droned on, "I need to ask these questions. Have you . . ."

She got the letter but not the spirit.

We later watched the same idiocy being repeated with an elderly woman who did not speak English. As if a ninety-year-old, ninety-seven pound woman meets the profile of a terrorist! Worse, the agent insisted that the young couple who accompanied the woman ask the questions and translate for her. Give me a break!

The problem? Management, of course! Obviously, this was a case of an employee being told the how but not the why. Stupid training and stupid policies cause stupid service not stupid employees.

This Blooper Award goes to any organization that follows policy blindly without thinking about how it might impact the customer.

☞ Too Busy: Awarded for Placing the Customer Last.

Comment: When you buy anything, certain services are included. They may not be itemized on your bill but they are there nonetheless.

While researching my next book, *Borrowed Dreams,* I worked as a carnie; you know, the folks who run the rides and food and games at carnivals. This carnival, my carnival, was part of the Do Da Festival in Chandler, Arizona.

Story:

I had been working for hours. The temperature was said to be one hundred and three. It felt like two hundred by the time I was given a break.

I wandered into a fast-food restaurant just off property. My hands were filthy and the idea of a clean restroom and running water was a good one.

Because the line was so long, I decided to order and then wash. Good idea. Would have worked, too, if the restaurant's management had not decided to lock the restrooms. Instead of serving their guests, this crew had decided to lock them out, providing instead two very hot portable toilets set against the building.

(Remember the movies where they punish the prisoner by locking him in a box on the desert? Same thing.)

"Excuse me. I just ordered lunch and would like to wash my hands."

"Sorry, our restrooms are closed."

"Yes, I know. But I've seen your employees unlock them to use and I'd like to use them, too."

"Sorry, they're closed. Use the outside ones."

"There is no running water in the portable toilets and my hands are dirty. Where can I wash?"

"You can't. We closed the restrooms because we are too busy."

Let's see if I have this straight. If business is slow, clean restrooms are included. If the customer honors you with lots of business, so much that you could afford to hire someone to do nothing but monitor the restrooms, all you get is the desert torture box. Do I have that right?

This Blooper Award goes to all those places that think that there is such a thing as a captive customer.

THE POS PROMISE

If there has been one unanswered question about Positively Outrageous Service, it has been over the issue of just what does a POS organization do. Positively Outrageous Service is not an idea that can be regimentalized. You can't put it in a box. In fact, putting POS in a box is a certain way to kill it.

Several years ago we presented to a major international corporation and were thrilled with the response. Thrilled that is until a few weeks after the presentation when we received a copy of a letter sent to their branch managers worldwide. In essence, it proclaimed that this corporation had committed to being a POS kind of place. Good news. But then it went on to list opportunities to deliver POS and commanded the exact response that would be approved. Bad news.

Positively Outrageous Service is of the moment and from the heart. It cannot be systematized, regimented, or otherwise formalized. There is no formula for Postiively Outrageous Service. However there are a few things that you can say about a POS organization. Here they are:

- You will be served not sold. No high-pressure selling or gimmicks, ever.
- Your order will be right. Or it will be made right, no hassles, no questions.
- You will be served by competent folk who care. We'll hire and train the best. To back this up, POS organizations have in place a system for measuring customer

satisfaction and responding quickly when service standards fall.

Because so many really terrific service organizations have adopted POS as their mantra, we've created a signature marketing program that allows them to use the POS service mark to tell their customers that they practice POS and are recognized as being among the very best service providers anywhere. When you see the POS service mark, you can rely on service that meets the standards listed above.

Caution: When you proclaim Positively Outrageous Service, even if you are not approved to use the POS service mark, you are raising the bar. Customers will automatically hold you to a higher standard. What you want to avoid is raising the expectation of a service surprise that will serve, not sell. Promise that you will get things right no matter what. Promise carefully selected and well-trained staff. But don't promise a surprise. Do that and you are creating standards that will be impossible to meet.

For more T. Scott Gross . . . www.tscottgross.com

Work hard. Play hard. Serve hard.
And don't forget
to love one another.

T. SCOTT SPEAKS

To arrange for T. Scott Gross to present to your group as a keynote speaker or trainer, please call 800-635-7524 or contact via web site: www.tscottgross.com or e-mail him at tscott@hctc.com

INDEX

ABOUT THE AUTHOR

A storyteller by nature, T. Scott Gross is one of America's most interesting and entertaining platform performers. In the business world, T. Scott is known for his insistence that work and living are supposed to be fun. The expert on relationships whether business, consumer or personal, T. Scott offers simple but elegant tactics for getting things done.

Photo by Phelps/Gredell Studios

T. Scott writes and speaks from experience. Like most of his readers, T. Scott knows what it's like to meet a payroll. With the heart of an adventurer, T. Scott is a hands-on guy who jumps into life and work with both feet. He is a devoted dad and husband who usually travels with his best friend on the planet, the love of his life, his co-pilot and partner—Melanie.

For more T. Scott Gross . . . www.tscottgross.com